Pick 'n' Mix

Over 100 ideas to create programmes for children of all ages!

Judith Merrell

Scripture Union

Welcome to Pick 'n' Mix!

To help you use this book the contents have been divided into ten sections, each containing ten ideas. You can **pick** activities from any section in the book and then **mix** them up with two or three other ideas to create your own tailor-made programme. At the end of the book, you will find ten sample programmes showing how ideas can be combined to provide well-balanced, half-hour activity sessions.

Contents

Scripture Union, 207–209 Queensway, Bletchley, MK2 2EB, England.

First published 1997, reprinted 1998, 1999, 2002

ISBN 1 85999 096 7

British Library Cataloguing-in-Publication Data
A catalogue record for this book is available from the British Library.

Cover design and illustration by Blue Pig Design Company.

Printed and bound by Ebenezer Baylis & Son Ltd, The Trinity Press, Worcester and London.

Scripture Union
We are an international Christian charity working with churches in more than 130 countries providing resources to bring the good news about Jesus Christ to children, young people and families – and to encourage them to develop spiritually through the Bible and prayer.

As well as our network of volunteers, staff and associates who run holidays, church-based events and school Christian groups, we produce a wide range of publications and support those who use resources through training programmes.

1 Ten ideas for icebreakers

A WARM WELCOME!

It's always a good idea to think about how you welcome the children to your group, even on a week by week basis. What's the atmosphere like when they first arrive? How do you think they feel? One simple way of breaking the ice and creating a warm and friendly atmosphere is to have a tape of lively music playing. Even adults find it easier to chat when there is background music, perhaps because they don't feel as if everything they say is going to be overheard. If you have an overhead projector, why not put up a sign that says 'Welcome', or one or two jokes, or perhaps the relevant notices for the week. It's always good to make those coming feel they are expected. If possible, get to your group a few minutes early so that you have everything ready and can spend a few minutes chatting to them before the programme begins.

ICEBREAKERS

Icebreakers are simply a good way to help your group get to know each other. If you meet with your group every week, you won't want to use an icebreaker every time. However, you might want to use one at the beginning of a new term, on the first day of a holiday club, or at a party where you have a large number of visitors.

1 Yes/No Challenge

As the children arrive, give them three pasta shapes each. Other small objects will work equally well, eg paper-clips, dried peas. Pair up the children, but ask them to change partners every couple of minutes. You may need to ring a bell or blow a whistle as a sign for them to change. The aim is for the children to interview their partners and to find out as much about them as they can. The only rule is that no one is allowed to say yes or no, and they must not nod or shake their heads. If a child does any of these things, he must give one of his pasta shapes to his partner. The child who has gained the most pasta shapes at the end of the game wins.

2 Number Clusters

Play some lively music and encourage the children to run or dance around the room. Every so often, stop the music and call out a number less than ten. The children then organise themselves into groups of that number. Give the groups a simple task before you start the music again, eg 'Find out the middle name of everyone in your group' or 'Find out everyone's favourite television programme'. Repeat the game using different numbers and different questions. Any children who are unable to make a group of the right number must sit out until the number of players out is the same as the number called by the leader. A wise leader will make sure that no one is left to sit out too long!

3 Make a Party Hat

It's often difficult to join a big group and start chatting; but if you have something to do with your hands or something you can talk about, joining in is immediately less daunting.

Give each child two large sheets of newspaper, one sheet of coloured paper and three paper-clips. The children use these to make their own special hats or party hats. Have some quiet music playing in the background and, while the group is working, take the opportunity to go round and have a few words with each child. Ask the children to think of a suitable title for their hat, and finish with a silly hat parade.

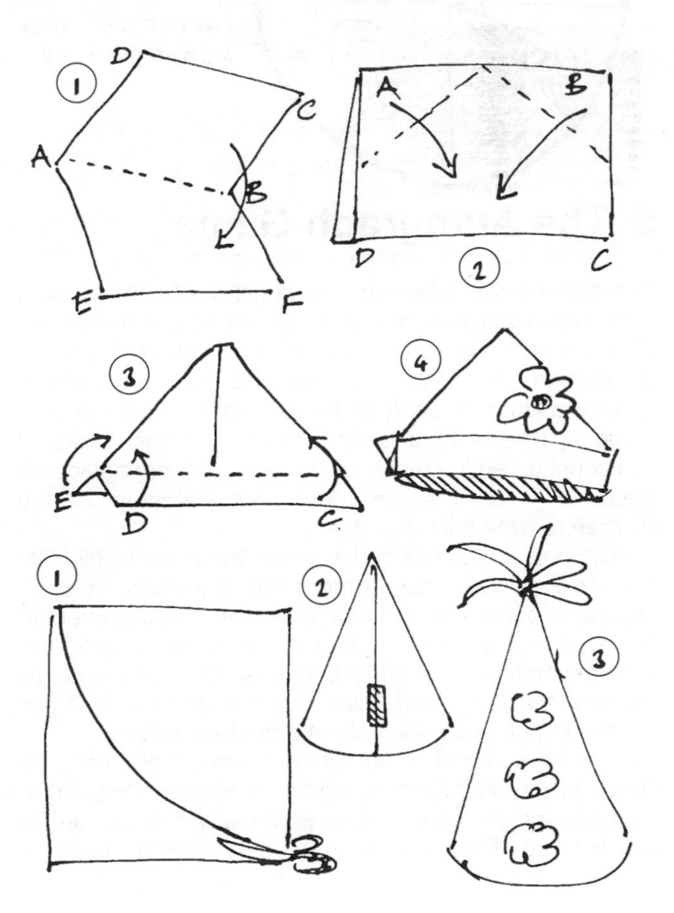

4 Make a Shield

As the children arrive, give out felt-tipped pens and large paper shield-shapes. Explain that you want them to make their own personal shield (see illustration). In the top left corner they must draw their family, and in the top right corner their favourite hobby. The strip across the middle is for their name. In the bottom left corner they should draw an achievement they are proud of, eg learning to skateboard, passing a piano exam, keeping their bedroom tidy for a whole week! Finally, in the bottom right corner they should write a quality they would love to be known for, eg patience, kindness, cheerfulness, generosity, a good listener. Make sure the children understand that this is a quality they aspire to, so they don't need to feel embarrassed about discussing their own personal qualities.

When everyone has finished, take a look at all the shields and let the children explain what they have drawn and why. If you have a large number of children, it would be a good idea to break up into smaller groups to discuss the shields.

5 The Autograph Game

This game works well with a large group of children, as it encourages everyone to mingle. On an A4 sheet of paper, draw a large square and divide it into a grid of 20 smaller squares. In each of the small squares, write a statement general enough to apply to three or four children in your group: eg 'I have a pet rabbit', 'I'm wearing white socks', 'I can count to ten in French', 'I ate toast and marmalade for breakfast'. Leave space under each statement for the children to write their signatures.

Photocopy enough of these to give one to each child. Tell the children they must collect the signature, in each square, of someone who can agree with the statement in that square. It's important that the statements given are fairly general, so as to provide a reasonable chance of all the squares being filled. Insist that the children don't ask anyone to autograph their sheet more than twice.

If you have used The Autograph Game before, you may like to try this slightly more advanced version. Write 20 or so more specific questions to which only one person fits the bill: eg 'Find someone whose middle name is Jemima'; 'Find someone with a dog called Shep'; 'Find someone who climbed the Eiffel Tower last May'; 'Find someone who bought a pair of Wellington boots last week'. When players find the correct individual, that person will write one or two letters of the alphabet in the relevant square (told her beforehand), so that players can eventually spell out a mystery phrase or the location of the prize, eg 'You've won an extra jelly at tea time!' or 'Look for a small red box'. With younger children you will want to supply the letters in the correct order, while older children might enjoy the challenge of a set of anagrams.

6 Step into the Picture

On the photocopier, enlarge the picture on p 6. It will be most effective if you copy the picture onto acetate so that it can be displayed on an overhead projector, but if this isn't possible enlarge it to A3 size. The picture shows a cartoon group in action, and many of the things happening will be mirrored in your own group. Use it to help you get to know the children better and to facilitate discussion.

Begin by asking them to take a minute to study the picture. Then explain that you want them to imagine they are one of the people in it. Use the following questions to stimulate a short discussion:

Which of the people in the picture is most like you? Why?
If you could be anywhere in the picture, where would you like to be?
If you could be anyone in the picture, who would you be?
Do you think that you would be happy to be part of that group? Why?
If you could change something that's happening in the picture, what would you change?

7 Parachute Games

A play canopy or parachute is great fun to use with children of all ages. Many parachutes come with a booklet of suitable games, but here are just a couple to get you started.

Up 'n' Under

Lay the parachute down on the floor and get the children to make a circle around the outside. They should all have enough space to be able to stand and hold the parachute with both hands. Invite the children to help you slowly waft the parachute up and down. You may find that it helps to raise and lower it to a count of four.

When everyone has got the hang of this, explain that as the parachute is going up you are going to call out a particular category: anyone who fits this category must run under the parachute and find a new place on the other side. You might like to use some of the following categories:

Anyone wearing jeans
Anyone who supports Manchester United
Anyone who has had a bath this week!
Anyone who ate cornflakes for breakfast
Anyone with brown eyes
Anyone wearing something red

Anyone who watches *Home and Away*
Anyone with a birthday this month
Anyone who likes chocolate
Anyone who hates football

With older children, a leader can walk round the outside and whenever he or she taps someone on the shoulder that child can shout out the next category. If you decide to do this, it's a good idea to warn the children at the beginning so that they have already thought of something.

PARACHUTE FOOTBALL

Once again, gather the children around the outside edge of the parachute. Divide the parachute into two halves or teams. Ask the children to stretch the parachute out so that it is taut. Then throw a lightweight football into the centre so that it sits on the hole in the middle. On the blow of a whistle, the two teams must raise, lower and generally jiggle their side of the parachute to try and flick the ball over the heads of the opposite team and so score a goal. Team members aren't allowed to throw the ball with their hands or to head it. After each goal, position the ball on the central hole again. Continue until one team has scored ten goals, or play to a fixed time-limit.

8 Choosers

You probably made Choosers when you were a child! Photocopy the one on p 7 (enough for each member of your group) and cut them out. If possible, use coloured paper. Fold back the four outside triangles along the bold lines, so that they meet and form a square on the other side. Now fold in the next four triangles along the dotted lines so that the point of each one reaches the star in the centre. At this point you should find that only the numbers on the front and the colours on the back are visible. Turn your Chooser over, fold it in half and then into quarters, and finally open out these last two folds. You should now be able to insert the finger and thumb of your right hand under Red and Yellow and the finger and thumb of your left hand under Blue and Green. Push the four colours together so that they are now at the top of your Chooser. As you open and shut your fingers and pull them from side to side, the numbers inside are revealed.

Invite the children to walk around and chat to each other using the Choosers. First, each child asks the person she meets to choose a colour, and spells out the letters of that colour by opening and shutting the Chooser. Next, the other person chooses a number from the four that are revealed. Again, the Chooser is opened and shut the equivalent number of times. Finally, the other person chooses another number from the four shown. The child opens up that number and reads out the question for her partner to answer. Encourage the children to use their Choosers to speak to as many people as possible.

9 Zoo Halves

Prepare a set of 'animal cards' by writing the first half of a word on one card and the second half on another card, eg GIR-AFFE, LI-ON, RAB-BIT, ELE-PHANT, ANTE-LOPE, HAM-STER, PAR-ROT, DON-KEY, CAM-EL, TI-GER. As the children arrive, attach half a word to their backs. The children have to attempt to identify what animal they are by asking the rest of the group questions like 'Am I furry?' 'Do I have a tail?' 'Am I fierce?' 'Do I have stripes?' The other members of the group have to guess which animal the half-word represents and to answer the questions as accurately as possible. A leader can always be called in to help anyone who runs into difficulties. Once a child has worked out which animal he is, he must then find his other half.

10 Who Has the Answer?

On a photocopier, enlarge the symbols on p 8, cut them out individually and stick them up around the walls of your meeting room. Write the meanings of each symbol on individual sticky labels and put a label on each child's back. If you have more than twenty children, you may like to create a few more symbols so that everyone can be included. On the other hand, if you only have a small group, put more than one label on each child.

Give each of them a pencil and paper, and get them to write down the numbers 1 to 20. They then walk round the room, look at the symbols and write down *not* the answer but the name of the child with the correct answer on his back! In this way the children will need to mingle and find out each other's names. If you have a wide age range, allocate an older child to help a younger one. At the end, bring the children back together to check their answers.

ANSWERS

1 Wool
2 Dollar
3 Roadworks
4 Information
5 Water
6 Percentage
7 Please recycle, or Recycled
8 No entry
9 No smoking
10 Icthus/Christian fish
11 Cycle route
12 Put litter in the bin
13 Worldwide Fund for Nature
14 Danger – falling rocks
15 Poison
16 Hand wash only
17 Price bar-code
18 No dogs
19 Highly inflammable
20 Dangerous substance

The principle of putting clues/questions on the walls and the answers on the children's backs can be used for many different games: picture clues relating to Bible stories, famous faces with the eyes blacked out, famous people and the names of the TV programmes they star in.

STEP INTO THE PICTURE

CHOOSER

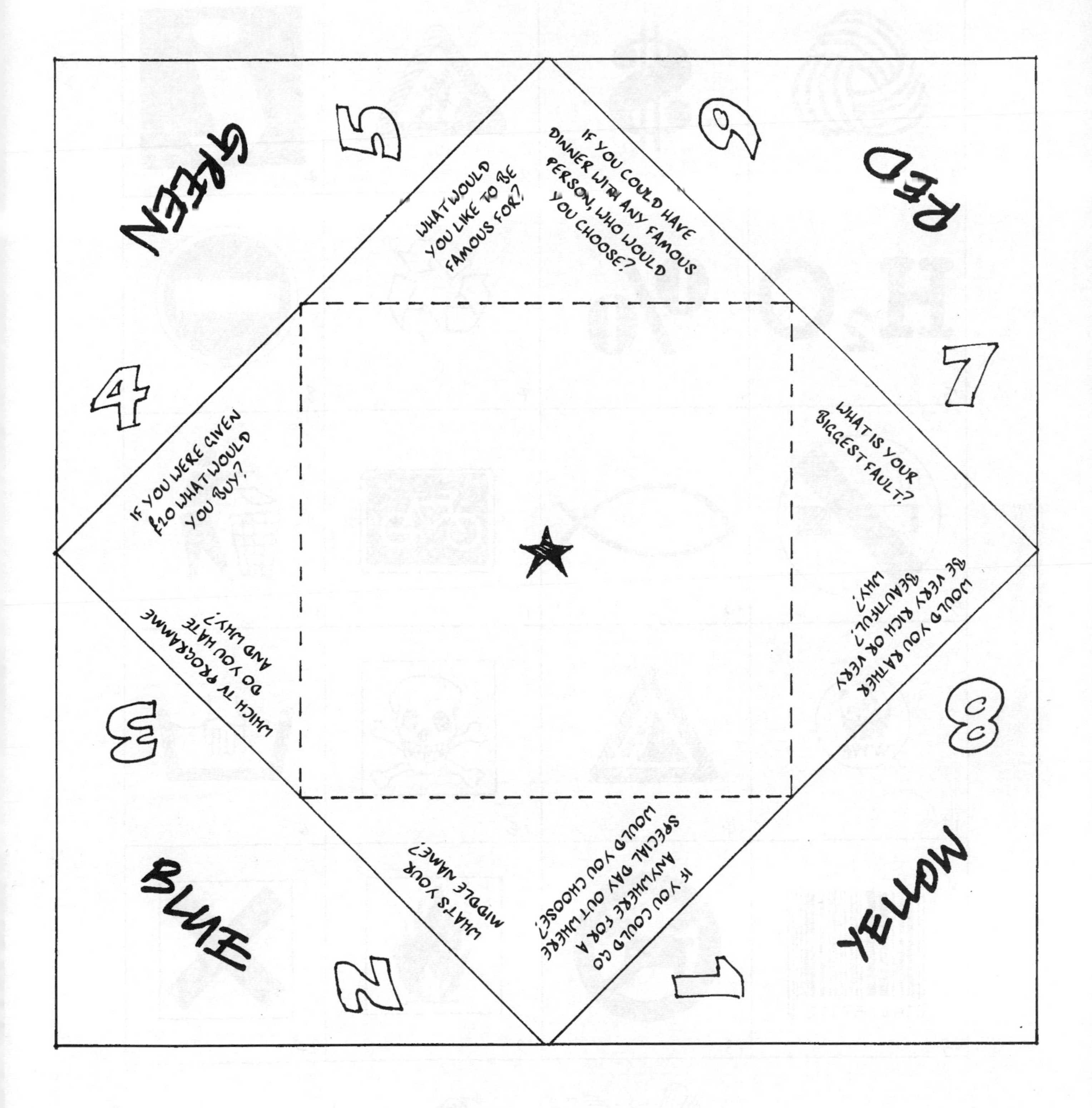
GREEN
RED
YELLOW
BLUE
1
2
3
4
5
6
7
8
WHAT WOULD YOU LIKE TO BE FAMOUS FOR?
IF YOU COULD HAVE DINNER WITH ANY FAMOUS PERSON, WHO WOULD YOU CHOOSE?
WHAT IS YOUR BIGGEST FAULT?
WOULD YOU RATHER BE VERY RICH OR VERY BEAUTIFUL, WHY?
IF YOU COULD GO ANYWHERE FOR A SPECIAL DAY OUT WHERE WOULD YOU CHOOSE?
WHAT'S YOUR MIDDLE NAME?
WHICH TV PROGRAMME DO YOU HATE AND WHY?
IF YOU WERE GIVEN £10 WHAT WOULD YOU BUY?

WHO HAS THE ANSWER?

2 Ten ways of telling a Bible story

There's no such thing as someone who can't tell stories. With a few tips and tricks, and lots of practice, everyone can learn to tell a story that children will enjoy. Let's look at the why, where and how of storytelling.

WHY?

The Bible is full of so many exciting stories: about shipwrecks, battles and romance; about kings and queens, families, journeys, weddings, amazing adventures and exciting escapes. It contains stories which appeal to all tastes, which are worth telling just for the enjoyment of hearing them. However, if we decide to include a Bible story in our programme, it's a good idea to have an aim in mind. A Bible story can teach us so much about God, it would be a shame to waste the opportunity of helping children to understand a little more about him.

Jesus told stories to help people understand the many things he wanted to teach them, so we can follow his example. Through the parable of the good Samaritan he taught people that it's right to treat everyone as a neighbour. He used the parable of the rich fool to help them think about the folly of materialism, and the parable of the lost sheep to help them understand the extent of the Father's love for every individual. We can retell Jesus' stories, and we can tell others about Jesus, about people who came before him and those who came after him. Whatever story we choose, we need to stop and think what God might wish to show the children through that particular story. Thus we may want to tell the story of the storm on the lake to show that, just as the disciples turned to Jesus when they were afraid, so we can do the same. If we choose the story of Zacchaeus the tax collector, perhaps our aim might be to explain how knowing Jesus can change our lives.

WHERE?

Now let's think about *where* you tell a story. This might sound a little strange if you meet in the same room every week! However, once in a while you can stimulate extra interest in a story by choosing an appropriate setting. For example, you could tell the story of Mary and Martha in the hall kitchen, so that you can mimic Martha busily preparing the meal. You could tell the story of the feeding of the five thousand while you are all sitting on the grass outside, so that the children can identify with the crowd. The story of the wise men could be split into sections and written on the back of numbered stars which are then pinned up around the room. The whole group can then follow the star to discover the story.

If your group normally sit on chairs, you need to think about how these are arranged. In Picture 1 (p 10), the back row would find it difficult to see because they are placed directly behind the row in front. In Picture 2, the chairs are staggered so that the children in the rows behind will be able to see through the gaps in the chairs of those in front; but it's possible that those sitting on the end of the row will find their attention wandering towards the windows or the pictures on the walls. Picture 3 shows the chairs arranged in a semi-circle so that everyone is facing the storyteller. A semi-circle also feels more friendly and less regimented.

Don't forget that when small children sit on big chairs their legs go to sleep, which makes them wriggle and fidget. It's also worth remembering that if you stand up to tell the story, you may be towering above the children, which means they get a crick in their necks just watching you! With younger children you might like to sit with them on the floor, so that they can easily see you and your visual aids. These things may seem very mundane, but once the children are comfortable they will concentrate better.

HOW?

Here are fourteen tips about some of the things worth doing or not doing when you tell a story to a group:

- ☞ **Don't** ask the children to read aloud verse by verse. This spoils the flow of the story and embarrasses less confident readers. Moreover, bright children will probably be preoccupied with silently practising their verse beforehand, counting the verses and calculating the number of children in the row who will read before them. As a result they miss the beginning of the story!
- ☞ **Don't** make your story too long. Junior-age children can only give their undivided concentration to something for five to ten minutes. Sadly, they don't all choose the same five to ten minutes to concentrate!
- ☞ **Don't** read aloud to your group (unless you absolutely have to!). If you bury your nose in a book, you'll lose eye contact with your audience, which is an important element of storytelling. Most children prefer a story to be told rather than read.
- ☞ **Don't** use too many long and difficult words. After all, how do you think a young child would interpret words like Pharisee, Samaritan, prodigal son, prophet, Messiah, salvation, forgiveness? Prepare your narration in advance and build in an explanation of any strange words or concepts.
- ☞ **Do** pray, prepare and practise aloud beforehand. (That's easy to remember – they all begin with the letter P!)
- ☞ **Do** have a clear aim or objective in mind.
- ☞ **Do** tell the children that you'll be asking a few questions at the end. The promise of a quick quiz does wonders for their concentration!

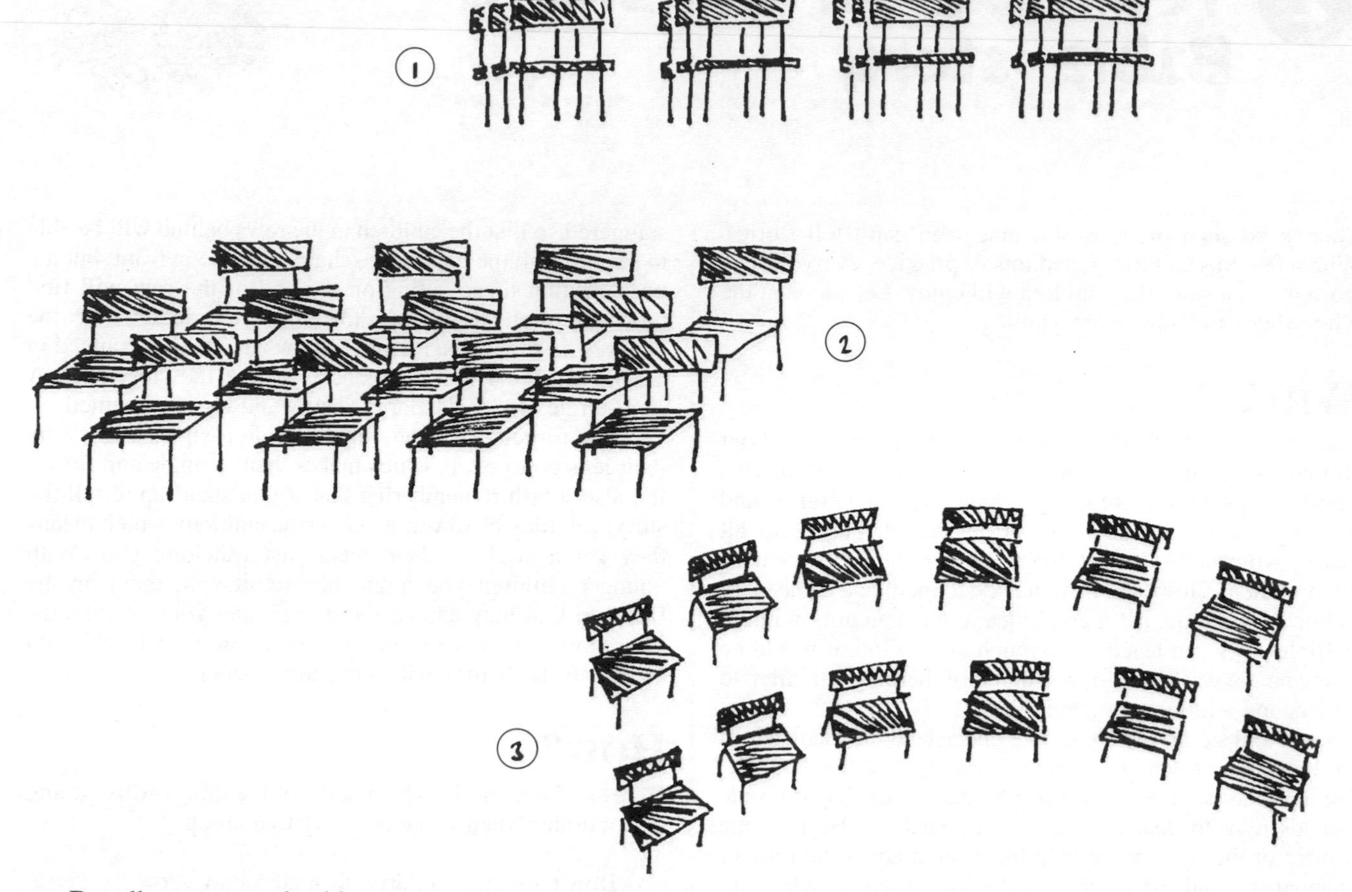

- **Do** tell your group that it's a true story. In an age when children regularly watch the miraculous exploits of fictitious superheroes like Batman, the Power Rangers, Superman and Dr Who, it's important that they know that Bible stories are true and we can believe in the miracles performed by Jesus. We can use stories about Jesus to show the children that he is a real hero who is well worth following.
- **Do** begin with an exciting opening, build towards a climax and finish with a thought-provoking end.
- **Do** use visual aids. Pictures, puppets, OHP acetates and the like, all act as memory triggers. Research has proved that children are far more likely to remember a story if they have been shown pictures or other visual aids. Don't forget that *you* are the best visual aid of all! Don't be afraid to use plenty of gesture, facial expression, movement and mimicry. You may even want to dress up as a biblical character to tell your story.
- **Do** use plenty of variety in your voice. Aim to vary the pace, pitch and power of your voice and don't be afraid to pause for dramatic effect. (Another four things beginning with the letter P!)
- **Do** use plenty of action and conversation. They will ensure that your story moves at a fast pace.
- **Do** try to find an interesting angle on your story. Older children, who greet every story with 'We've heard this one before ...', may enjoy hearing a familiar story from a new angle. Try telling the story of Jesus walking on water from the point of view of the astonished fish, the story of Zacchaeus from the point of view of the groaning sycamore tree, the story of the feeding of the five thousand from the point of view of two starving sparrows who were disappointed to see all the leftovers being collected up. The possibilities are endless!
- **Do** build your message into the story. If you finish and then say, 'And this story teaches us that ...', you'll find the youngsters have all stopped listening. As far as possible, let one of the characters in the story draw out the teaching point.

1 Picture Story

A story with accompanying pictures is one of the most popular methods of storytelling. If you have a group that is easily distracted and inclined to look out of the window, you'll find that a series of pictures will help to focus their attention at the front of the room.

Pictures can also help children to understand the story. The story of the four friends (who lowered a sick man through a hole in a roof to see Jesus) sounds extremely dangerous and highly improbable if you imagine a modern Western house with a sloping roof! A picture showing a biblical house with a flat roof and outside stairs goes a long way towards explaining the story. My four-year-old nephew couldn't quite make sense of the story of Zacchaeus counting taxes. He had misunderstood his group leader and imagined Zacchaeus counting his taxis! Again, a picture would have made all the difference.

You may want to draw your own pictures, or you may prefer to photocopy something out of a book. *How to Cheat at Visual Aids!* (Scripture Union) contains over five hundred pieces of photocopiable artwork covering the majority of stories in the New Testament. A second book, *How to Cheat at Visual Aids! (Old Testament)*, covers most of the earlier stories in the Bible.

It is always worth mounting your pictures on coloured card so that they appear to be framed. This will give them more emphasis and ensure that they aren't too floppy to hold up. And why not write some notes about each section of the story on the back of the relevant picture? Your notes will be hidden from view, but you will know they are there and, if you are a little nervous about telling stories in public, the notes will give you extra confidence.

The following sample story is based on Luke 2:8–20, in which the angel Gabriel tells the shepherds the good news about the birth of Jesus. Enlarge each of the four pictures on p 19 to A4 or even A3 size to show to your group. If possible, take a little time to colour them in – you could always enlist the help of a child.

Picture 1:
Josh held out his hands towards the crackling bonfire to warm them. It was a chilly night and he was glad to be with his friends, Obed and Dan. All the sheep were safely gathered together and settled for the night in their sheepfold. The shepherds knew they could rely on the bright bonfire to scare any wild animals away. So now the three young men were whiling away the time telling stories and exchanging news.

Picture 2:
Suddenly there was a great blaze of light and a man in bright, shining clothes appeared. To their astonishment, the shepherds realised that the man was an angel. Josh felt his knees knocking. He couldn't help feeling rather frightened – the angel looked very imposing. However, the angel seemed to understand just how they were feeling. He smiled at them all and said, 'Don't be afraid! I am here with wonderful news for you which will bring great joy to everyone. Today, in Bethlehem, your Saviour was born – Christ the Lord! And this is what will prove it to you: you will find a baby wrapped in strips of cloth and lying in a manger.'

Then, just as the shepherds were getting used to the presence of one angel, a whole army of heaven's angels appeared, all joyfully singing praises to God.

'Glory to God in the highest heaven and peace on earth to those with whom he is pleased,' they sang in splendid harmony. The shepherds knew they had never heard anything quite so beautiful before.

Picture 3:
When the angels had left and gone back to heaven, the three shepherds discussed all they had seen and heard.

'Well I never!' said Obed. 'God actually sent his own angel to give us an important message. It's not as if we were anyone special – we're only shepherds. But the angel came to *us*.'

'You're right there!' agreed Josh. 'And since God sent the message, I think we should go straight to Bethlehem to see this little baby.'

'Well, what are we waiting for?' said Dan in a rush to get going. So the three shepherds rolled a huge log across the entrance to the sheepfold, just in case the sheep should try to wander off, and set off for Bethlehem.

Picture 4:
It wasn't long before they reached the little town, and there they found the baby Jesus lying in a manger in a small stable at the back of an inn. They met Mary and Joseph and shared with them all the angel had said about their baby son. Jesus slept peacefully in the manger while everyone talked about him.

'Aahh! Isn't he beautiful?' cooed Dan.

'Yes, he's certainly a very special little chap,' replied Josh. 'I reckon that we're really fortunate to be among the first people to see him.'

After the shepherds had admired Jesus and congratulated Mary and Joseph, they said their farewells and left the little family.

'I've just got to tell someone what happened to us tonight. It was so exciting,' said Josh, bubbling over with happiness. 'The sheep will be all right for a while longer. Let's go and tell our friends and families this amazing news.'

So Josh, Dan and Obed set off for home. They were so happy, they couldn't help praising God with a cheerful little song that they made up as they walked along the road.

2 Balloon Characters

Story figures are fun to make and there are many different types. For example, you might want to twist together two pipe cleaners to make a little figure to show the children as you tell the story. Pipe-cleaner figures can be dressed in scraps of material and made to bend and move as appropriate to the story. Alternatively, you could draw your own Bible characters and paste the pictures on lengths of kitchen roll tube, so that they stand on a table (see illustrations, p 12). The possibilities are endless!

Balloon characters are something a bit different and the children always enjoy playing with them at the end of the meeting. Blow up a balloon to represent each character in your story, then cut out a large pair of feet from heavy cardboard for each one. Attach the feet to the knot at the base of the balloon and you will find that the weight ensures that, even if the balloons are thrown in the air, they always return right side up. Once you have attached a pair of feet to each balloon, use sticky shapes and marker pens to add other features. You will find that with a little ingenuity you can also attach paper hats and even tea-towel head-dresses to your balloon figures. The finished figures look not unlike the ever-popular Mister Men!

Balloon figures work particularly well for the story of the two house builders, Matthew 7:24–27 and Luke 6:47–49. Perhaps you might choose a long blue balloon for the wise man and a round orange balloon for the foolish man! You could also attach their respective houses to balloons, and fix a cardboard disc to the base of these so that they stand upright. You can then burst the balloon behind the foolish man's house at the appropriate point in the story.

You might like to use the following sample story.

Introducing Mr Wise and Mr Wally

Many years ago Jesus told a story about two house builders. Let's pretend that they were called Winston Wise and Walter Wally.

Now Winston *(show first balloon character)* was a very thoughtful, hard-working young man. He had saved up his money for many years, taken plenty of advice and planned his house very carefully. He spent a long time selecting just the right spot and eventually decided to build his house on a foundation of solid rock. 'A good foundation is very important,' he said to himself, 'and I want my house to last a very long time.' So Winston started to build his house. He measured everything carefully and followed his plans to the very last detail. Before long he had completed the foundations.

Now Walter Wally was a very different character *(show second balloon character)*. One morning he decided to build himself a new house, and before lunch he had bought the land and ordered the bricks. Walter loved swimming so he decided to build his house close to the sea, *very* close to the sea – in fact, he decided to build it on the beach! He sketched a few plans on the back of an old envelope, and before the day was over he had already built two of the walls of his house. So there they were – Winston Wise and Walter Wally, one building slowly and carefully, the other building fast and furiously.

Before long both houses were finished and ready to live in *(show houses)*. Winston and Walter moved their furniture into their respective houses, and they were both highly delighted with their brand new, thoroughly modern homes. The sun shone, the flowers bloomed and the birds sang. Life was wonderful!

Then, one day, a fierce storm blew up. So Winston and Walter went inside their houses, shut their front doors and waited for it to blow over.

But the storm grew worse. The rain bucketed down, the thunder crashed and the lightning flashed all around. Winston Wise was cosy and snug inside his house, but poor Walter Wally was beginning to feel rather frightened. His house was leaking and creaking, and he was starting to get rather wet. In fact, he only just abandoned his house in time before it crumbled and tumbled and fell to the ground with a deafening rumble of falling bricks *(burst the balloon supporting Walter's house)*.

Fortunately, Winston was looking out of his window just as poor, bedraggled Walter came paddling by, so he invited him in for a mug of hot chocolate.

'It's very strange,' said Walter, sipping his chocolate, 'that your house is still standing while mine collapsed! I just can't understand it.'

'Well,' said Winston, 'it's all to do with foundations. I built my house on solid rock, but you built your house on the sand.'

Do you know? Our lives are a bit like houses. If we listen to Jesus' words and obey him, then we'll be like Winston Wise building on a firm foundation. But if we listen to Jesus' words and do nothing about them, then we'll be like Walter Wally – a right idiot! Wouldn't you rather be wise than wallyish?

3 A Story with Sound Effects

Many of the stories in the Bible lend themselves to being retold with added sound effects. Children enjoy participating in stories, and the fact that they may be called on at any moment to provide a sound effect helps them stay alert and concentrate.

The following example is based on the storm on the lake, Mark 4:35–41. All the sound effects have been printed in ***bold italics*** in the text. It is a good idea to practise some of them beforehand so that the children understand what they are being asked to do. Take care to actually 'act out' the sound effects rather than just read the words in italics. If another leader is available, you may want to write out the sound effects on individual sheets of A4 paper and ask the other person to hold up each one at the appropriate point in the story. Alternatively, make each sound effect yourself and ask the group to copy you. In the style of an orchestra conductor, use a hand gesture to invite the group to join in with you, and hold your hand up when you want them to stop.

The Storm on the Lake

It was towards the end of a long day and we were all feeling pretty tired. ***(Yawn!)*** Jesus suggested that we take the boat over to the other side of the lake, so I helped a couple of the others to push the boat out. ***(1,2,3, Push!)***

It was lovely sailing across the lake. The evening air smelt good and we could hear the birds calling to each other as they flew home to roost. ***(Tweet, tweet, tweet!)*** All day Jesus had been working hard, preaching and teaching. He was so tired that he was already fast asleep in the front of the boat. ***(Snore!)***

It was really crowded in the boat, but I managed to lie down and stretch myself out for a rest. I felt tired, but happy. ***(Mmmm! Aaaahhh!)*** The sun was setting on the horizon as I shut my eyes and dozed off. ***(Snore!)***

However, it wasn't long before I woke up with a start! Our little boat was pitching and tossing, and the wind was blowing really strongly now. ***(Puff and blow!)*** I looked down and saw that my feet were in a pool of water. The waves were splashing thick and fast over the sides of the boat. ***(Splish, splash!)*** I felt so scared that my knees were knocking and my teeth were chattering. ***(Chatter, chatter!)***

All the other disciples were awake now. We were feeling very cold ... ***(Brrrr!)*** And very scared ... ***(Oooh errr!)***

'Are we going to be shipwrecked? Is the boat going to sink?' we asked each other. ***('Is the boat going to sink?')***

Then I looked to the front of the boat and was amazed to see that Jesus was still fast asleep. ***(Snore!)***

The wind was blowing ... ***(Puff and blow!)*** The waves were splashing ... ***(Splish, splash!)*** And Jesus was fast asleep! ***(Snore!)***

I went over and woke him up. 'Master, Master, don't you care that we're going to be shipwrecked?' I asked. Jesus stood up in the boat. He saw the strength of the waves ... ***(Splish, splash!)*** He heard the power of the wind ... ***(Puff and blow!)*** And he said in a commanding voice, 'Be calm! Be still!' And the wind died away and the waves were calm. It was amazing! I looked at the other disciples, and we all said to each other, 'Who is this man?' ***('Who is this man?')***

For at that moment we all realised that Jesus even had power over the wind and the waves. Jesus is certainly someone very special. Nothing is too difficult for him.

4 A Story with Responses

Younger children love to participate in a set response to a story. The fact that the same phrase comes up over and over again gives them confidence and adds to their enjoyment. Where possible, add a special tone of voice and perhaps a hand gesture to add to the effect. The following example is based on the story of the lost sheep, adapted from Luke 15:1–7 and Matthew 18:12–14.

The response is divided into two parts: 'But though he searched with greatest care/He couldn't find Larry anywhere'. Whenever the leader says the first half of the phrase (in *italics*), the children join in with the second half (in ***bold italics***), although by the end of the story they should be able to join in with the whole line. As you say the words 'greatest care', put your hands to your eyes as if searching all around; and when you say 'he couldn't find Larry anywhere', open your hands to show they are empty. Try to emphasise the rhyme in the words 'greatest care' and 'anywhere', as this will help the children remember the line. The last two responses in the story introduce a slight variation. Say these loudly and clearly, and you will find that the children will join in anyway.

Larry, the Lost Lamb

Once there was a shepherd who had a hundred sheep. He was a very kind man and he looked after his flock very well. If they were hungry he led them to green grass, and if they were thirsty he took them to cool streams. Every evening he carefully counted his sheep as they came into the fold to sleep. Then he would lie down across the entrance to stop any wild animals getting in.

One rather cold night he was counting in his sheep as usual: '...'96, 97, 98, 99...' Only 99! One was missing. He double-checked, but again he could only count 99. Larry, the youngest and whitest lamb in his flock, wasn't there. The shepherd looked in every nook and cranny of his sheepfold.

*But though he searched with greatest care/**He couldn't find Larry anywhere.***

The poor shepherd was feeling very tired, but he knew that he had to go and search for his precious lamb. He climbed over rocks and squelched through mud.

*But though he searched with greatest care/**He couldn't find Larry anywhere.***

He was feeling rather damp and very cold. But he loved his little lamb so he carried on looking. He looked under every bramble and behind every thorn bush.

*But though he searched with greatest care/**He couldn't find Larry anywhere.***

Every few minutes he called out to his precious white lamb, 'Larry, Larry! Where are you?' But there was no reply, not a single bleat, so he carried on looking. He searched every hill and every valley.

*But though he searched with greatest care/**He couldn't find Larry anywhere.***

The hours passed, and daylight was beginning to creep across the sky. The shepherd realised that he had been searching for Larry all night and he still hadn't found him. 'No matter how long it takes, I'm not going to give up,' thought the shepherd to himself. So he carried on looking and looking and looking.

*But though he searched with greatest care/**He couldn't find Larry anywhere.***

Then, from behind a distant rock, he heard a very faint bleat. As he went towards it, the noise got louder and louder and louder – until he looked behind the rock and there was Larry stuck in a thorn bush, wriggling with all his might. The shepherd put his arms round the lamb and pulled, gently but firmly.

Then, when Larry was free, he popped him inside his jacket where the little lamb was warm and snug, and set off to walk all the way back to the sheepfold. Larry bleated contentedly as the shepherd tickled his ears. 'Do you know? I was really worried about you because...

'*...though I searched with greatest care/**I couldn't find you anywhere.***

'I'm so very happy that I've found you.'

The next day the shepherd invited his friends and neighbours round for a party to celebrate because he had found his lost lamb. He told them, 'I'm really happy to have found my precious little lamb. I was so sure that I'd lost him because...

'*...though I searched with greatest care/**I couldn't find Larry anywhere.***'

Our Father God loves us just as much as that shepherd loved his sheep. He comes looking for us and reaches out to us. Every time someone new becomes a member of his family there's a great big party in heaven to celebrate.

5 Stand up, Turn round, Sit down

If you have trouble making your group sit still while you tell them a Bible story, why not channel their excess energy into an active story-time? Divide the children into groups and name each group after one of the characters in the story. Whenever they hear that character mentioned, they must stand up, turn round and sit down again as quickly as possible. This may sound chaotic, but in fact the children listen to the story very attentively, waiting for the next time their character is named.

The following example is based on the story of Mary and Martha, Luke 10:38–42. Before you start, divide the children into three groups, to represent **Mary**, **Martha** and **Jesus**. This active approach seems to fit in well with the idea of Martha rushing around doing the cooking and cleaning.

Jesus had two special friends called **Mary** and **Martha**. They lived in a little village with their brother Lazarus. **Mary** and **Martha** always worked very hard. Every day they collected water from the well. Then **Martha** would make fresh bread while **Mary** washed the clothes in a nearby stream. Later, **Mary** would milk the goat and **Martha** would turn the milk into cheese. **Mary** and **Martha** kept a very tidy house where there was always a warm welcome and plenty of home cooking.

One day **Jesus** sent a message to say that he was coming to visit and that he'd like to bring some of his disciples with him. The two sisters were delighted. **Jesus** was a good friend and they always enjoyed seeing him. **Martha** spent hours in the kitchen kneading bread and stirring soup, baking cakes and churning butter. She wanted to prepare a wonderful meal for **Jesus**. Meanwhile, **Mary** concentrated on the cleaning. She dusted the house from top to bottom, swept the floors and washed the linen. She wanted the house to be clean and tidy for **Jesus** and his friends.

When the day arrived, the two sisters rushed to the door to welcome **Jesus** and his disciples. Then **Martha** went back to the kitchen to give her soup another stir and to give the floor an extra sweep. She had to be sure that everything was just right for **Jesus** and his friends, and she was beginning to feel rather hassled. 'Now where's **Mary**?' thought **Martha** to herself. 'I really need her here helping me. I'm trying to cook a meal for all these people and **Mary** goes and disappears.'

Martha looked out of the window and saw **Mary** sitting with **Jesus** and his friends under a big shady tree, listening intently to everything he had to say. 'Hmm, that's just not fair!' she thought to herself. 'Here am I working my fingers to the bone, and **Mary** is just sitting listening to **Jesus**. She should be helping *me*.'

Martha banged her pots and pans in the kitchen. She got more and more upset until she couldn't stand it any longer. She stomped outside, walked straight up to **Jesus** and grumbled, 'Don't you care that I'm doing all the work while my sister just sits here with you?'

Jesus didn't react in the way **Martha** expected him to. Instead he looked at her kindly and said very gently, '**Martha**, **Martha**, you are worried and troubled about the cooking and cleaning, but at this moment **Mary** knows that it is more important to sit and listen to me.'

Martha stopped in her tracks. She realised that she had wasted the first hour of **Jesus**' visit, and she felt rather foolish. However, everyone was very kind. **Mary** helped her serve the supper, and everyone complimented her on the truly tasty meal. Then the disciples helped with the washing up, so Martha had some extra time to spend with **Jesus**.

That night, as **Martha** went to bed, she realised that she had learnt a very important lesson. Listening to **Jesus** is more important than housework – much much more important!

6 Time to Act

Why not try writing a sketch with your group? Choose a Bible story with a good story-line and a clear beginning and end. One of the parables or a story about someone Jesus met would probably work best. If you plan to perform the sketch, you'll need to ensure that the story comes across loudly and clearly. Try using two or three narrators to explain the action and keep the story moving. Keep the narrators' lines short so that the pace is maintained, and don't be afraid to split a sentence between two or even all of the narrators. Long speeches tend to make a sketch slow and tedious, and create problems for young readers. The narrators can stand at microphones on either side of the acting area and read their lines from clipboards.

Once you have written the basic script and chosen the narrators, take another look at the story and work out how much of the action can be mimed by the remaining group members. A story with a crowd in it gives you the opportunity to include the whole group! If you would like to give the crowd one or two lines but don't have much time to rehearse, you could write their lines on large cue cards which can be held up by someone sitting in the front row. An added advantage to this style of sketch is that if someone is ill on the day of your performance, with a few adjustments, the show can still go on.

For added effect, dress the narrators in similar costumes, eg they all wear jeans, red T-shirts and baseball caps. Or ask the actors to wear T-shirts or sweatshirts of a similar colour – this helps to create the impression of a troupe of actors. If you need to use props, the bigger and brighter the better.

The following example is based on the story of Zacchaeus, Luke 19:2–9.

A Change for the Better

Characters:

- Two narrators who read their lines from clipboards
- Zacchaeus and Jesus who both mime their roles
- The crowd who mime the action and read their lines from large cue cards

Scene:
Jericho, the town centre. The narrators stand down stage left and right. Zacchaeus, the crowd and Jesus are centre stage.

1: This is the story –
2: Of a mean and nasty man –
1: Called Zacchaeus.
(Enter Zacchaeus. The crowd hiss and boo.)
2: He was a devious fellow.
(Zacchaeus pulls mean and nasty faces and rubs his hands together in eager anticipation.)
1: An odious fellow –
2: A dubious fellow –
1: A contemptuous fellow.
2: In other words –
1: He was a mean and nasty man!
2: Zacchaeus lived in the town of Jericho –
1: Where he was a tax collector –
2: A chief tax collector.
1: And he was a rich man –
2: A very rich man.
1: But whenever he went into the town –
2: All the people used to run and hide.
(Zacchaeus approaches the crowd, but they all back away.)

Crowd: Be careful watch out!
Zacchaeus is about!

1: Zacchaeus wasn't an honest tax collector.
2: He used to cheat the people out of their money –
1: By taking more than he should –
2: And keeping huge sums for himself.
(Zacchaeus mimes counting out his money.)
1: 'One for the Romans and two for me.'
2: 'One for the Romans and three for me.'
1: 'A little for the Romans and lots for me.'

Crowd: Zacchaeus is so mean and greedy,
He steals money from the poor and needy.

2: One day when Zacchaeus walked into town –
1: Everyone was far too busy to run and hide.
(The crowd chats excitedly.)
2: In fact they were so busy –
1: That they totally ignored him.
(Zacchaeus approaches several groups, but they turn their backs on him.)
2: A very special person was visiting the town.
1: And his name was Jesus.

Crowd: Wave the flags and shout, 'Hello!'
Jesus is in Jericho!

2: Zacchaeus very much wanted to see Jesus.
1: In fact, he was desperate to see Jesus.
2: But he just wasn't tall enough.
1: He jumped up and down behind the crowd –
(Zacchaeus mimes jumping.)
2: But he still couldn't see.
1: Then he tried to crawl through their legs –
(Zacchaeus mimes crawling.)
2: But he was so fat that he got stuck.
1: And then he had a good idea.
2: Close at hand was a sycamore tree.
(Two or three members of the crowd make a tree shape. If your 'tree' is not strong enough to support the weight of Zacchaeus, position a chair just behind the 'tree'.)
1: So Zacchaeus decided –
2: To climb into its branches.
(Zacchaeus mimes climbing tree.)
1: And a few minutes later Jesus arrived.
(Enter Jesus.)
2: Everybody cheered and waved –
(The crowd cheers and waves.)
1: They knew that Jesus was a very special person.
2: Then Jesus walked straight to the sycamore tree.
1: He looked up into its branches –
2: And said –
1: 'Hurry down, Zacchaeus' –
2: 'Because I must stay in your house today.'
1: Zacchaeus was so astonished –
2: He nearly fell out of the tree.
(Zacchaeus comes down from the tree in a great hurry.)
1: 'How does Jesus know *my* name?'
2: 'Why does he want to come to my house?' –
1: He said.
2: All the people in the crowd were equally astonished.
1: 'How does Jesus know his name?'
2: 'Why does he want to go to *his* house?' –
1: They said.
(The crowd shake their heads and mutter as Zacchaeus leaves with Jesus.)
2: And they started to mumble –
1: And grumble –
2: Moan –
1: And groan.

Crowd: It's just not fair!
Why has Jesus gone there?

2: Some time later –
1: Zacchaeus returned –
(Re-enter Zacchaeus.)
2: With outstretched arms –
1: And outspread hands –
2: A spring in his step –
1: A smile on his face.
2: 'Listen everyone!' –
1: He said –
2: 'I'm going to give half my belongings to the poor.'
1: 'And if I've cheated anyone' –
2: 'I'll give back twice' –
(Zacchaeus rushes round handing out money.)

1: 'No, three times' –
2: 'No, four times' –
1: 'As much as I took.'
2: The change in Zacchaeus was quite astonishing.
1: His meeting with Jesus had changed him –
2: Utterly –
1: And completely.

Crowd: Zak's no longer horrid and mean –
He's the kindest man you've ever seen!

2: And Zacchaeus was as good as his word.
1: He gave half his belongings to the poor –
2: And gave back all the money he'd stolen –
1: With interest.
(Pause.)
2: Then he made a fresh start –
1: As a friend of Jesus.

Crowd: Hooray!
(If the children playing the crowd are old enough, let them let off a few party poppers at the end of the sketch.)

7 Acetate Story

An overhead projector is a wonderful tool for a youth worker. A small acetate can be enlarged on the screen so that a church full of people can see the picture. Acetates can be used over and over again, and are slim, lightweight and easy to store – a distinct advantage over enormous pieces of artwork which can only be stored under the spare-room bed! Pictures can be traced or photocopied onto acetate, and those in black-and-white can be printed easily and cheaply. Most photocopy shops will also make coloured acetates, which is worth the extra cost and effort if the pictures are to be used on several occasions.

An overhead projector screen may be used a bit like a puppet theatre, since characters can be made to walk on and off the screen. Attach a strip of clear acetate to the bottom of each figure to enable you to gently push or pull them so that they slide across the screen. Since acetate figures are largely transparent, a figure that walks on from one side can be flipped over so that he is pointing in the right direction to return home!

It is also possible to make things appear and disappear as if by magic. Use sticky tape to attach additional pictures to the edge of your main piece. These are folded out of sight at the beginning of the story, but can be flipped onto the screen at the appropriate moment. In this way Gabriel appears before Mary, or flames materialise suddenly over the disciples' heads at Pentecost.

Our sample story is based on the good Samaritan, Luke 10:30–37. Photocopy the artwork on p 20 and attach strips of clear acetate to any figures you want to slide across the screen as though they are walking or riding (in particular the priest, the Levite and the Samaritan on his donkey). Introduce and remove characters as the story progresses.

Disaster on the Road to Jericho

One morning Jesus was explaining to one of the teachers from the Temple that he must love his neighbour. But the teacher wasn't quite sure that he understood. 'Who exactly is my neighbour?' he asked Jesus in a puzzled tone. Jesus answered the question with a story, and this is the story that he told.

It was a bright and sunny day, and a traveller was making his way from Jerusalem down to Jericho. *(Slide Picture 1 half way across the screen.)* He was feeling rather tired after his stay in the city, and he was glad to be out in the open country. He breathed in the fresh air and hummed a little song to himself as he walked along.

All of a sudden, as he came round a bend in the road, three fearsome robbers pounced on him. *(Replace Picture 1 with Picture 2.)* They took his cloak and his tunic, his sandals and his moneybelt, then beat him up and left him for dead. *(Replace Picture 2 with Picture 3.)*

'Oh my poor head!' thought the traveller to himself as he lay beside the road in the hot sunshine. Every bone in his body ached and he was unable to even crawl, let alone walk. 'Oh dear, oh dear!' he groaned. 'I'll just have to lie still and wait for someone to come to the rescue. I do hope they come soon.'

Before long a priest came walking round the bend in the road. *(Slide Picture 4 across the screen towards Picture 3.)*

'What luck!' thought the traveller. 'He'll certainly help me.' But, to his complete astonishment, the priest took one look at him and crossed over to the other side of the road. *(Stop Picture 4 half way across the screen, then move it to the bottom and off the screen.)*

'Poor man!' thought the priest to himself. 'But I'd better not stop. I don't want to get my hands dirty on the way to the Temple. Besides, those robbers might just come back!'

A short while passed and then the traveller heard another set of footsteps. He raised his aching head and saw that it was a Levite on his way home. *(Slide Picture 5 across the screen towards Picture 3.)* The Levite came right up to the traveller and took a good look at him. Then he hurried away muttering, 'Oh dear! What a shame! Sorry I can't stop! Must rush!' *(Stop Picture 5 half way across the screen, then move it to the bottom and off the screen.)*

The poor traveller was feeling pretty grim by now. 'Whatever will become of me? If no one stops, I'll surely die!'

Just then another man came round the bend in the road. *(Slide Picture 6 across the screen towards Picture 3.)* He was from Samaria. 'Well, I'm sure *he* won't stop,' thought the traveller. 'Jews and Samaritans don't get along too well at the best of times.'

But, to his astonishment, the Samaritan came right up to him and said kindly, 'You poor chap! Where does it hurt? Let me see what I can do to help you.' *(Replace all previous pictures with Picture 7.)*

The Samaritan took some oil and wine to clean and soothe the traveller's wounds. When he had finished bandaging him up, he put him on his donkey and took him to a nearby inn. *(Replace Picture 7 with Picture 8.)* He gave the innkeeper two silver coins and asked him to take good care of the traveller while he was getting better. 'And when I come back,' he added, 'I'll pay you whatever else you spend on him.'

When Jesus finished his story he said to the teacher, 'Now which of the three men do you think acted like a neighbour to the traveller?'

'Why, the one who showed kindness!' answered the teacher.

'Exactly!' said Jesus with a smile. 'Now you go away and behave just like him.'

8 Mime Time

It's always fun to mime a story. When it comes to mime the confident children who enjoy acting are put on a more even footing with the shy ones who hate to speak in public, since no one is allowed to talk. The added advantage is that it can turn a noisy group into a silent one!

Choose an exciting story where there is plenty of movement, and write a narration where each action is described step by step for the children to mime. Invite the children to find a space where they will have enough room to turn round without bumping into anyone else. A leader then reads the story aloud, leaving pauses for the children to mime the relevant actions.

The following mime is based on the story of Jesus and Peter walking on water, Matthew 14:22–32. In this story the children are invited to mime Peter's actions and reactions.

Peter Splashes out in Faith

Peter yawned and stretched. ***(Pause.)*** It had been a long day and he was feeling pretty exhausted. The little fishing boat was bobbing up and down on the waves and Peter was finding it hard to stay upright. ***(Pause.)*** He wobbled a little and then sat down with a bump in the bottom of the boat. ***(Pause.)*** He put his hand to his eyes and peered out into the blackness. ***(Pause.)*** It must have been around four or five in the morning and it was far too dark to see anything properly.

The wind was blowing even more strongly now, and the waves were crashing against the sides of the boat. Peter wrapped his cloak tightly around himself. ***(Pause.)*** He was beginning to feel pretty chilly. ***(Pause.)*** He looked around at the other disciples. ***(Pause.)*** They were all wide awake – the boat was rocking too hard to let anyone fall asleep. Peter was even beginning to feel ever so slightly sea-sick! ***(Pause.)***

Then one of the disciples pointed out into the darkness and said, 'What's that?' Peter stood up to get a better look. ***(Pause.)*** He swayed a little from side to side. ***(Pause.)*** So he grabbed hold of the mast of the boat to steady himself. ***(Pause.)*** In the distance he could see someone or something walking on the water towards the boat. 'Perhaps it's a ghost!' cried one of the disciples. Peter felt his fingers trembling. ***(Pause.)*** And his knees knocking together. ***(Pause.)*** He was beginning to feel rather afraid.

Suddenly, out of the darkness, they heard a voice saying, 'Courage! It is I. Don't be afraid!' Immediately they realised that the figure was Jesus. He seemed to be walking on the water, *actually walking across the surface*!

Then Peter cupped his hands around his mouth and called, 'Lord, if it's really you, order me to come out on the water to you.' ***(Pause.)*** 'Come on then!' replied Jesus.

Peter opened his mouth in amazement. ***(Pause.)*** Why ever did he make such a crazy suggestion? He couldn't walk on water! Then he looked at Jesus, and very carefully he put one foot and then the other foot over the side of the boat. ***(Pause.)*** He put his arms out to steady himself. He was standing, actually standing, on the water. ***(Pause.)*** 'This is quite amazing!' thought Peter. Then he fixed his eyes on Jesus and put one foot in front of the other. ***(Pause.)*** Slowly, step by step, he moved towards Jesus. ***(Pause.)*** 'This really is incredible!' thought Peter. 'I'm walking on top of the water.'

With great interest Peter looked all around him. ***(Pause.)*** He saw the waves crashing at the side of the boat. He heard the strong wind blowing. And he began to feel rather nervous and frightened. ***(Pause.)*** First his toes and then his feet and ankles started to feel wet. ***(Pause.)*** He was sinking down into the water! ***(Pause.)*** At this point Peter was feeling really scared. He turned his eyes back to Jesus and shouted, 'Save me, Lord!' ***(Pause.)*** At once Jesus reached out and grabbed hold of him. Then they walked back to the boat together.

'Oh Peter, how little faith you have. Why did you doubt?' asked Jesus. Peter climbed back into the boat without answering. ***(Pause.)*** He would always remember how, with Jesus holding his hand, his fears had vanished and he had immediately felt confident. With Jesus anything was possible.

The other disciples in the boat had watched the whole scene with their mouths wide open. They looked at Jesus. They knew he was someone very special. 'You are certainly the Son of God!' they exclaimed in wonder. Peter quietly nodded his head in agreement. ***(Pause.)***

9 Changing Feelings

If you decide to tell a story with visual aids, it's often hard to find enough time to draw all the different pictures you need to represent each stage of the story. This idea enables you to draw just one figure but to add on a whole range of different expressions. You'll notice that our simple Bible figure (p 21) looks rather like the shape of a keyhole, so it's very easy to copy! Draw your own figure, but give the face a neutral expression so that you can use *Blu-tack* to attach different expressions as the story progresses.

Our Bible story is based on John 20:19–29. In this story we hear how Thomas's feelings changed from sadness to bewilderment and, finally, joy. For your convenience the story has been divided into four sections, and each change of expression has been printed in **bold** type. Present the figure of Thomas in (i), then add the three changes of expression as they are marked in the text.

i) Meet Thomas. He was one of Jesus' twelve disciples. Thomas followed Jesus as he travelled through different towns and villages. He heard Jesus preach and teach, and he witnessed many amazing miracles. Thomas counted Jesus as his very best friend.

ii) But one terrible Friday something happened that spoilt everything. Jesus was put to death on a cross even though he had done nothing wrong. Thomas felt **sad and miserable**. Without Jesus, life would never be the same again.

On the following Sunday evening the disciples gathered together; but Thomas decided that he'd rather be alone, so he took himself off for a long walk. While he was gone, Jesus suddenly appeared in the room where the others were meeting. They were amazed and overjoyed to see him alive again. He had died on the cross and been buried, but three days later here he was living and breathing and standing in the room with them. What a shame that Thomas wasn't with them! The disciples couldn't wait to tell him the good news.

iii) When Thomas returned, the disciples were so excited that they all started speaking at once: 'We've seen Jesus. He was here in this very room!' Thomas couldn't believe his ears. He felt **puzzled and bewildered**. He had seen Jesus' dead body laid in the tomb and the huge rock rolled across the entrance. He just couldn't believe his friends' amazing story. It was too good to be true. 'Unless I see the scars of the nails in his hands,' he said, 'and put my finger on those scars and my hand in his side, I will not believe.'

iv) A week later Jesus appeared to the disciples again, and this time Thomas was with them. Jesus looked at him kindly and said, 'Put your finger here, and look at my hands; then stretch out your hand and put it in my side. Stop your doubting, and believe!' Thomas was **overjoyed** to see Jesus again. He looked at his good friend and said, 'My Lord and my God!' because he knew that Jesus was someone very, very special.

Jesus said, 'You believe because you have seen me. Blessed are those who believe without seeing me.' This blessing still applies to all of us today who believe in Jesus without actually seeing him face to face. Isn't it good to know that we have our own special blessing?

10 Draw a Story

Children love to see pictures even if they are roughly drawn and scarcely a work of art! It's said that children first remember the pictures they see and then the story that goes with them, so visual aids work as an important memory trigger. You don't have to be Rembrandt to draw a few stick people while you tell a story, and it doesn't matter if the end result is only a simple sketch. Your group will love to see a picture grow before their eyes and they will get a great deal of pleasure out of watching an adult attempt to draw. You may even find that they offer the odd helpful hint!

Stick people are easy to draw provided you don't try to make them too complicated! Don't try to draw a neck, shoulders or hips on your stick person. Hands are only required if you want your character to hold something or point to something. Feet, however, are useful since they help to show in which direction the character is walking. It's worth trying to get the proportions correct and, if you try studying a friend, you should discover the following:

- The head and body together are equal in length to the legs.
- The arms are as long as the body and the hands reach to just below the top of the legs.
- The elbows come halfway down the arms and they point backwards.
- The knees come halfway down the legs and they point forwards.

Our sample story is based on Mark 10:46–52 in which Jesus heals blind Bartimaeus. To guide you, there are some simple stick-people illustrations on p 21. Practise in advance, then draw the pictures as you tell the story. If drawing isn't your forte, try sketching in a few faint pencil marks which are invisible to your audience but which you can see, and then draw over these.

A Bright Day for Bart

Picture 1:
As you tell the story, first draw Bart and then the crowd, including one small figure to represent the child. Finally, draw Jesus and add a speech bubble containing the word 'Jesus!' over Bart's head.

Bart was begging in the market place in the centre of town. Jericho was busier than usual and there were scores of people rushing about in all directions. Bart was blind so he couldn't see all the people, but he could hear their voices and sense their presence, and more than once someone trod on his hand or tripped over his foot. 'I wonder what's happening?' he thought. 'What's all the fuss about?'

Then he heard a small child say to his father, 'Can I sit on your shoulders so I can see Jesus when he arrives?'

'So that's what it's all about!' thought Bart. 'I wish I could see Jesus too.'

Bart remembered his father, Timaeus, telling him about Jesus only the week before, how Jesus had healed a paralysed man and helped another man who was deaf. A plan began to form in Bart's mind. 'I've got to meet Jesus. He will help me to see. I know he can heal me.' The noise of the crowd grew louder and louder. 'Jesus must have arrived,' said Bart to himself. He started to shout and shriek at the top of his voice, 'Jesus! Please stop! I need your help! Jesus! Jesus!'

The crowd around him were angry and tried to push Bart out of the way. 'Be quiet! Shut up! Jesus won't want to bother with a blind beggar like you!' But nothing would stop Bart shouting until finally he went hoarse with all his efforts. 'Oh dear! Jesus will never be able to hear me. There must be hundreds of people here. And I did so want to be able to see.'

Picture 2:
Draw Jesus, then add one or two disciples behind him. Finally, draw Bart standing in front of Jesus.

Jesus was some way away from Bart, but despite all the people crushing in on him he heard Bart call out his name. 'Someone's calling me,' said Jesus. 'Tell him to come here.'

Peter, one of Jesus' disciples, looked very puzzled. Who was Jesus talking about? There were hundreds of people everywhere and many of them were shouting and calling to Jesus. Peter followed Jesus' gaze and saw blind Bartimaeus. Soon the message flew out across the crowd from one person to another: 'Call Bartimaeus! Tell Bart to come here – Jesus wants him. Cheer up, Bart! Jesus has heard you calling him.'

Then Peter went over to Bart, helped him up and took him to see Jesus.

'What do you want me to do for you?' Jesus asked kindly.

'Teacher,' replied Bart, 'I want to see again.'

'Go,' Jesus told him. 'Your faith has made you well.'

At that moment the darkness covering Bart's blind eyes disappeared, and he looked into Jesus' face. He could see! He could actually see Jesus smiling at him, and the disciples grinning. He could see the crowd pushing closer so that they could watch what was happening. And he could see the bright coloured clothes everyone was wearing. This was truly amazing!

Picture 3:
Draw a picture of Bart with his eyes wide open, a huge grin on his face.

Bart looked at Jesus again. 'Thank you, Lord! Oh thank you so much! Please let me come with you. Wherever you're going, I want to go too!'

So Bart followed Jesus on his travels. Wherever he went he told everyone what an amazing miracle Jesus had worked for him and how Jesus had changed his whole life for the better.

PICTURE STORY
1
2
3
4

ACETATE STORY

CHANGING FEELINGS

DRAW A STORY

3 Ten ideas for quizzes

Quizzes and competitions are generally very popular with children, but take care that these don't become too competitive and just another way of affirming the bright children in the group. There will always be the enthusiastic ones who put up their hands and call out, 'Me, me, me!' But there are also some children who hate quizzes, fearing that their lack of knowledge will be made public. For this reason it's a good idea to let children answer in teams rather than to pick on individuals.

A quiz can be a good way of reinforcing Bible teaching, and children will often listen to the story more attentively if they think there will be a few questions at the end. If you like to have a quiz at the conclusion of several weeks' work, it's a good idea to include a few general knowledge questions for the sake of newcomers and children who are often away. Sadly, there are many children who can only come to Sunday groups every other week since they spend alternate weekends with an absent parent.

As far as possible keep the quiz short (five to ten minutes) and fast moving. Remember that if you have more than two teams children will have to wait quite a long time for their turn to come round, and when children get bored they start to fidget!

If you are working with a wide age range within one group, write some general questions but include a few specific questions for the different age groups, eg 'Here's a question for all those under six years old' or 'This next question is just for the ten-year-olds.'

If you only have a small group of perhaps two or three children so that team quizzes are impossible, try playing 'Beat the Leader'! For every quiz question the children answer correctly they score a point; a wrong answer means a point for the leader. Set a target at the beginning of the quiz, eg 'Can you beat the leader by scoring more than 7 out of 10?'

There are two types of questions that you can ask: closed questions where there is just one possible answer, and open questions where the answer is open to discussion. A typical closed question might be 'What job did Zacchaeus do?' Answer: he was a tax collector. A typical open question might be 'How do you think Zacchaeus felt before he met Jesus?' Answers might include 'Lonely', 'Miserable', 'Wealthy', 'Greedy'. Then later in the quiz you could ask, 'How do you think Zacchaeus felt *after* he had met Jesus?' It's a good idea to include a few open questions in a quiz to give children the opportunity to discover and discuss the meaning of a Bible story.

1 True/False Quiz

For this quiz, you will need to write ten or more statements based on the Bible story you are looking at. The children should be able to respond to each statement with the word 'True' or 'False' (see the examples given). Label one end of your room 'True' and the other end 'False'. Then invite the group to come and stand in the middle. Read out the statements one by one, and ask the children to indicate their response to each by running to the appropriate end of the room. Bring everyone back to the middle after each statement, and check that everyone knows the correct answer. With younger children it's fun to introduce variations! For each statement, suggest a different mode of travel so that the group might hop, skip, jump, run, walk backwards or even crawl to the relevant end of the room.

If your meeting room is too small for running around, divide the children into small groups and give each one a 'True' and a 'False' sign. Read out the statements and let the groups discuss and hold up the sign they believe indicates the correct answer.

The following True/False statements are based on the story of Jesus healing blind Bartimaeus, Mark 10:46–52.

1. Bartimaeus' father was called Timothy. *(False – he was called Timaeus)*
2. Bartimaeus lived in Jericho. *(True)*
3. Bartimaeus was very keen to see Jesus. *(True)*
4. The people in the crowd helped him by taking him to Jesus. *(False – the people scolded him and told him to be quiet)*
5. Jesus didn't hear Bartimaeus calling to him. *(False – despite the huge crowd Jesus heard Bartimaeus' voice)*
6. Bartimaeus had a great deal of faith in Jesus and he believed that Jesus could help him. *(True)*
7. Jesus asked the blind man, 'For how long have you been blind?' *(False – he asked Bartimaeus, 'What do you want me to do for you?')*
8. Bartimaeus said to Jesus, 'Teacher, I want to see again.' *(True)*
9. Jesus said to Bartimaeus, 'Go, your faith has made you well.' *(True)*
10. Bartimaeus was able to see immediately, and he rushed home to tell his parents. *(False – he followed Jesus on the road)*

2 Balloon Quiz

For this quiz you will need to write your questions on small slips of paper. Fold up the questions and push each one into a balloon. Blow up all the balloons and use a marker pen to label each one with the relevant question number. Invite children to come out, burst a balloon, extract the question and read it out for the group to answer. Just for fun you can suggest that each balloon be burst in a different way, eg by lying on it, sitting on it, jumping on it, squashing it between the knees, or even bursting it while standing back to back with a partner!

This quiz need not be competitive, although you can always divide the group into two teams and award points for correct answers.

3 Spot the Mistake

For this quiz you need to write a brief summary of your Bible passage or story and include a number of obvious mistakes. You can either read out the summary and ask the children to jot down all the mistakes that they notice, or you can give out typed summaries and let them work in small groups to find and underline all the mistakes. When everyone has finished, come back together to discuss and correct the story.

The following example is based on the story of the feeding of the five thousand, John 6:1–15.

A small crowd was following Jesus because they had seen him perform many incredible miracles. Jesus went up a hill and sat down with his disciples. Then he said to Philip, 'I want you to go to the supermarket and buy enough food to feed all these people.'

But Philip replied, 'That's impossible! It would take more than three hundred gold coins to buy enough bread for everyone.'

Then Andrew, a local policeman, said, 'There's a young girl here with five cakes and two apples, but that certainly won't be enough for all these people.'

Jesus told the disciples to ask the people to queue up. There were about five hundred men there. Then Jesus took the cakes, said a prayer of thanks and distributed them to the people sitting there. He did the same with the fruit.

When everyone had eaten enough, Jesus asked the disciples to gather up the leftovers. So the disciples collected the remaining food, and they filled ten boxes with all the leftovers.

The people who saw this miracle were quite amazed.

ANSWERS

A small ***(large)*** crowd was following Jesus because they had seen him perform many incredible miracles. Jesus went up a hill and sat down with his disciples. Then he said to Philip, 'I want you to go to the supermarket and buy enough food to feed all these people.' ***('Where can we buy enough food to feed all these people?')***

But Philip replied, 'That's impossible! It would take more than three hundred gold coins ***(two hundred silver coins)*** to buy enough bread for everyone.'

Then Andrew, a local policeman ***(one of Jesus' disciples)***, said, 'There's a young girl ***(boy)*** here with five cakes ***(loaves)*** and two apples ***(fish)***. But that certainly won't be enough for all these people.'

Jesus told the disciples to ask the people to queue up ***(sit down)***. There were about five hundred ***(thousand)*** men there. Then Jesus took the cakes ***(loaves)***, said a prayer of thanks and distributed them to the people sitting there. He did the same with the fruit ***(fish)***.

When everyone had eaten enough, Jesus asked the disciples to gather up the leftovers. So the disciples collected the remaining food, and they filled ten boxes ***(twelve baskets)*** with all the leftovers.

The people who saw this miracle were quite amazed.

4 Climb the Tree

For many Bible stories it's possible to choose something in the story to provide a scoreboard for your quiz. Thus for the story of Zacchaeus you could use a tree divided into ten stages, with a small figure of Zacchaeus for each team; with each correct answer, 'Zacchaeus' climbs higher up the tree. The winner is the first team to get their Zacchaeus to the top of the tree so that he can see Jesus.

For the story of the four men who climbed onto the roof, made a hole and lowered their paralysed friend down to see Jesus, you might like to draw a biblical house with about ten outside steps. For each correct answer the team move their counter one step nearer the roof.

For the story of the feeding of the five thousand, you might cut out simple paper baskets, one per team. Write seven questions for each team and award a paper fish or paper loaf for each correct answer, until one team has collected in their basket the five loaves and two fish mentioned in the story.

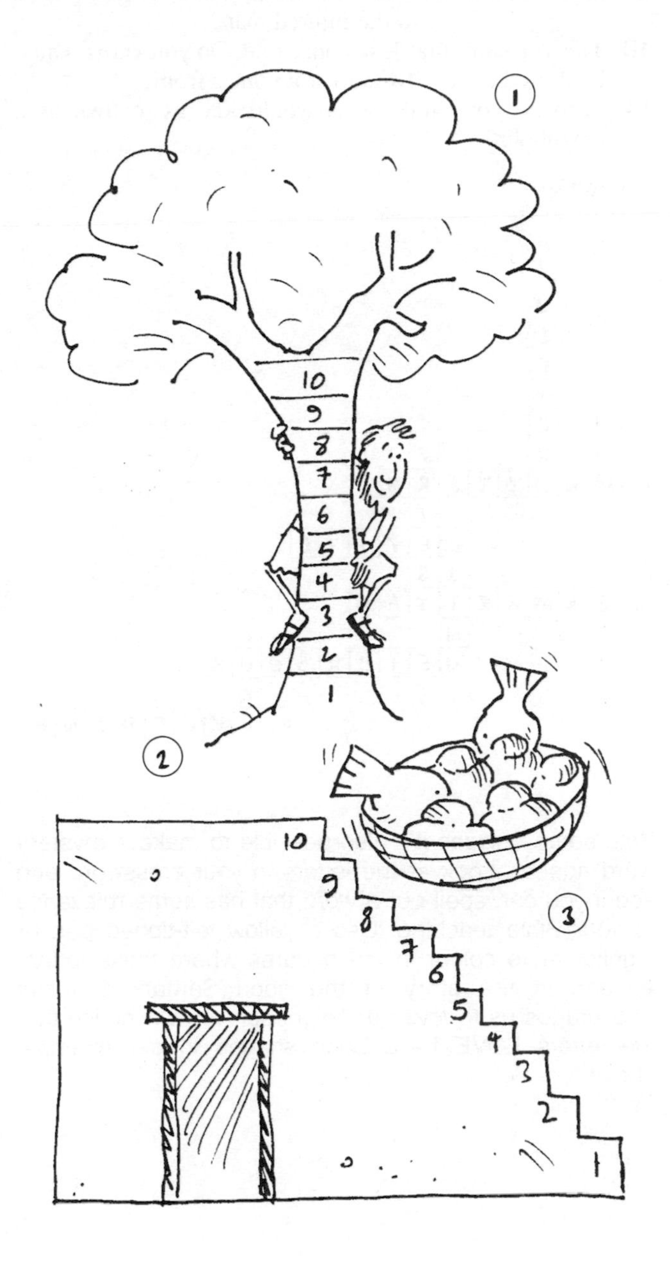

5 Crossword Quiz

Sometimes it's fun to create a crossword incorporating all the answers to the quiz questions. Using a marker pen, draw a giant grid on a large sheet of paper. Then each time a child answers a question correctly, he or she can come up and write the correct word in the grid. If you are working with teams, let each team write their answers in a different coloured marker pen.

The following example is based on the story of the good Samaritan, Luke 10:25–37.

QUESTIONS

1D Where was the traveller going?
1A Who attacked him?
2D Who first passed by on the other side?
2A Who went over to take a look at the traveller, then walked on by?
3A Who stopped to help?
3D Where did the Samaritan take the injured man?
4A Jesus asked, 'Which of these three acted like a _ _ _ _ _ _ _ _ _ _ to the injured man?
4D This is a story that Jesus once told. Do you know which book in the New Testament it comes from?
5A Who do you think Jesus would like us to treat as a neighbour?

ANSWERS

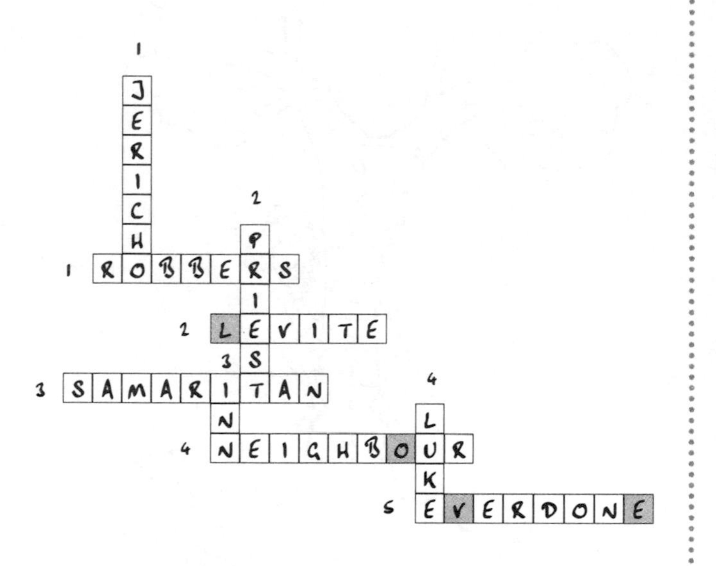

With some quizzes it's also possible to make a mystery word appear. Look at the letters in your crossword and see if you can spell out a word that has some relevance to your Bible teaching. Use a yellow felt-tipped pen or highlighter to colour in the squares where these letters appear. In the story of the good Samaritan Jesus encourages us to *love* our neighbour. You will notice that the letters LOVE have been shaded in our example above.

6 Roll the Dice

Quizzes often end with two teams having achieved identical scores. For older children this can be boring and predictable, so this quiz introduces an element of chance into the scoring system. The element of suspense generated by random scoring ensures that no child loses interest in the quiz, and keeps everyone sitting on the edge of their seat!

In 'Roll the Dice', every time a team answers a question correctly they can nominate someone to come out and roll the dice. The number on the top of the dice is their score for that question.

☞ TIP
An extra large dice is particularly useful for this quiz, and these can often be found in nursery education shops.

7 Blockbusters

This quiz is a variation on the popular television programme *Blockbusters*, and is probably best suited to older children. In this version, teams are faced with a four-by-four grid made up of hexagons, each containing a letter of the alphabet. Two teams (eg Stars and Triangles) take turns to choose one of the letters on the grid. One team works from top to bottom and the other from left to right. The leader reads out a question where the answer begins with that particular letter of the alphabet: for example 'What B is the place where Jesus was born?' *(Bethlehem)*, or 'Which S came and visited Jesus in the stable?' *(Shepherds)*. The team who raises their hands first, or is first on the buzzer, is given the chance to answer the question. When a question is answered correctly, remove that letter from the grid and replace it with a star or a triangle symbol, to show which team has won that hexagon. The first team to connect a line of hexagons wins.

Enlarge the hexagon grid, the sets of team symbols, and the alphabet letters (p 26), and photocopy them onto OHP acetate. Colour and cut out the symbols and letters (the grid is projected on a separate sheet of acetate). If you have more than one answer beginning with the same letter, you will need to photocopy an extra set of letters. Write sixteen questions based on the Bible story you are studying, and place the letters that match the first letter of each of your answers at random on the grid. Divide your group into two teams, and you are ready to begin.

The following *Blockbusters* questions have been based on the Christmas story, Matthew 1:1 – 2:15; Luke 1:1 – 2:20 (*Good News Bible*).

1. Which D was an ancestor of Joseph? *(David)*
2. Which G was an angel of the Lord? *(Gabriel)*
3. What I is another name for Jesus? *(Immanuel)*
4. What C was the reason why Joseph and Mary travelled to Bethlehem in Judea? *(Census)*
5. Which Z was father to Jesus' cousin? *(Zechariah)*
6. What R was Elizabeth to Mary? *(Relative)*
7. What N was the home town of Joseph and Mary? *(Nazareth)*
8. What J is the region where Bethlehem is situated? *(Judea)*

9 What M is a feeding trough for animals? *(Manger)*
10 Which S were visited by an army of angels? *(Shepherds)*
11 Which A sang 'Glory to God in the highest heaven'? *(Angels)*
12 Which H was king in Jerusalem at the time when Jesus was born? *(Herod)*
13 What W did the men from the east do when they found the baby born to be king of the Jews? *(Worship)*
14 What F was a special gift for Jesus? *(Frankincense)*
15 What T was the number of gifts brought by the visitors from the East? *(Three)*
16 What E was the place where Mary, Joseph and Jesus went to escape from Herod? *(Egypt)*

8 The Wet Sponge Quiz

This quiz can be played competitively or just for fun! Divide your group into teams and, if possible, allocate an adult team leader to each one. Write a number of quiz questions based on the Bible story or passage you are looking at. Then take a large sheet of cardboard and cut a hole in the centre, large enough for someone to poke their head through. When a team answers a question correctly, they can choose a member, or even the adult leader, from another team to come to the front and put her head in the frame. One of the team members then throws a wet sponge at her! If you are playing the quiz competitively, score 10 points for a direct hit on the face, 5 points for a hit on the cardboard frame, and no points for a miss!

The quiz works particularly well at holiday clubs or if you are meeting outdoors on a hot summer's day. Spread a plastic sheet on the floor if you are doing the quiz inside!

9 Pay a Forfeit

This is particularly popular with older children who often expect a quiz to be entertaining as well as challenging! Write a set of questions suited to the day's story and theme, then divide the children and adult leaders into two or more teams. Write the forfeits on slips of paper to be drawn out of a hat at random. For each question a child answers correctly, she can ask a member of the other team to pay a forfeit. But if she is unable to answer the question, then she must pay the forfeit herself! You may like to use some of the following forfeits, although you will doubtless be able to think of others that suit your group and meeting room even better.

1 Wear a blindfold and eat a small bowl of jelly with a fork. *(Blindfold the child and turn him around three times before you hand him the bowl)*
2 Kiss four bare legs. *(A discerning youngster will realise that a chair fits the bill!)*
3 With your hands behind your back, use your teeth to retrieve an apple from a bowl of water. *(A baby-bath filled with water is even more fun!)*
4 With your hands behind your back, use your teeth to retrieve a jelly baby from a bowl of flour.
5 With your hands and feet tied together, burst a balloon. *(The child will have to sit or lie on it)*
6 Walk backwards around the room, balancing a paper plate on your head and a plastic beaker full of water on top of the plate!
7 Use a pair of chopsticks to eat a small bowl of cornflakes. Don't forget to add the milk!
8 With your hands behind your back, unwrap and eat a wrapped sweet. *(After Eight mints work well)*

10 Penalty Shoot-out

This quiz contains an element of chance as in 'Roll the Dice'. Enlarge the ten footballs (p 27) on a photocopier, then cut them out. Stick the word 'GOAL!' on the back of six footballs and 'MISS' on the back of the other four, so that each ball can be turned over to reveal a result. You will also need to photocopy and cut out the goal net for each team. Attach the footballs to a board with *Blu-tack*, and fix up a goal net in front of each team.

Prepare ten or more quiz questions and ask them to the teams in turn. If the question is answered correctly, the team is invited to take a penalty shot. They then choose a football which is turned over to reveal whether they have scored a goal or a miss. Goals can be collected in the goal net. The winning team is, of course, the team with the most goals at the end.

BlockBusters

PENALTY SHOOT-OUT

4 Ten things to do with a sheet of paper or card

GETTING STARTED

If craft and chaos go hand in hand in your imagination, don't despair! Many of the items in this section are very quick and simple to make, and won't mean covering the carpet in glue, glitter and green paint! The secret of success is to be well-prepared. Make an example of the craft item beforehand so that the children will know what they are aiming at and so that you will know exactly how long it takes and which parts are a bit tricky where a little extra help might be needed.

Have everything ready before you start. Younger children may need to have all the cutting out done for them, so do this before they arrive. Older children will be able to cut out for themselves, but might need help with stapling, sewing or something similar. If you have a mixed age group, prepare things to a different stage for each child so that you have a sporting chance of everyone finishing at the same time.

Make sure you have plenty of newspaper or a large plastic sheet to protect the carpet, and have a roll of kitchen towel available to mop up any accidents. Men's shirts turned back-to-front and with the collars and cuffs cut off can make excellent aprons. You should be able to pick up dozens of cheap shirts in your local charity shop.

Children are creative and they love to make things they can take home at the end of a session. To avoid confusion, ask them to write their names on their 'creations' before they do anything else. It's very upsetting for a child to be told that her precious model or painting has got lost or gone home with someone else, and it's very embarrassing for a leader to have to explain this to the parents! For children from unchurched families a craft item can help bridge the gap between church and home. A child bearing a paper basket with five plasticine loaves and two fish will often go on to relate the Bible story to his parents. The child has an opportunity you may never have. For this reason it's often worth attaching a caption label to the back of a model or similar creation.

Younger children are always keen to take their creations home straight away, but older children can often be persuaded to let you display their work, and this can be a way of showing them how much you value what they have done. Don't forget to label each child's work with his or her name and perhaps even a title. An effective display will brighten up your meeting room, but it can also bring pleasure to others and be a source of information or a stimulus for worship.

☞ TIP

If you enjoy craft sessions with your group, but want some new ideas and fresh inspiration, try *Here's one I made earlier* by Kathryn Copsey (Scripture Union, UK price £5.99).

1 Windmills

You can make windmills just for fun, although if you want to give them a more practical use you could encourage the children to write one thing they want to thank God for on each point of the windmill and use them as part of your prayer time. An attractive display can be made by arranging all the windmills in florist's oasis and including a few sprigs of foliage.

☞ TIP

The need for drawing pins makes this activity unsuitable for use with very young children.

1. Take a square of white paper, and ask the children to colour a bright pattern on one side and a different pattern on the other side. Alternatively, use origami paper which is a different colour on each side.
2. Make four diagonal cuts in the paper, as shown.
3. Take the left-hand corner of each 'triangle' and bend it towards the middle. Fasten the four points to a piece of dowel with a drawing pin.
4. Blow gently on the windmill and, if the drawing pin hasn't been pushed in too tightly, it will whirl around.

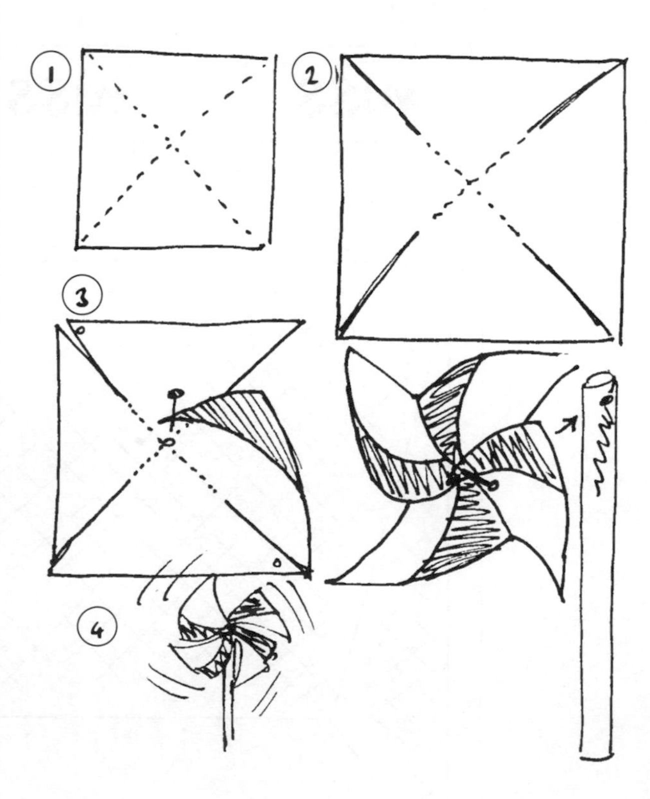

2 Helicopters

If you have never made paper helicopters with your group, you have got a real treat in store! They are easy to photocopy and very simple to make.

Helicopters are always popular with children and, since it is possible to write two or three lines of text along the shaft, they can be used effectively for invitations or messages. They are also an excellent means of helping children to learn a memory verse, so our second sample helicopter has been printed with the words of John 3:16.

1. Trace the helicopter outline onto a sheet of A4 paper. For a large group, you should find that you can photocopy five or six helicopter outlines on one sheet, provided you draw the helicopters facing in alternate directions.
2. Cut out the outline along the bold lines.
3. Attach a paper-clip to the nose. Fold one of the tail pieces forward and the other back along the dotted lines.
4. Drop the helicopter from a good height and watch it spin to the ground.

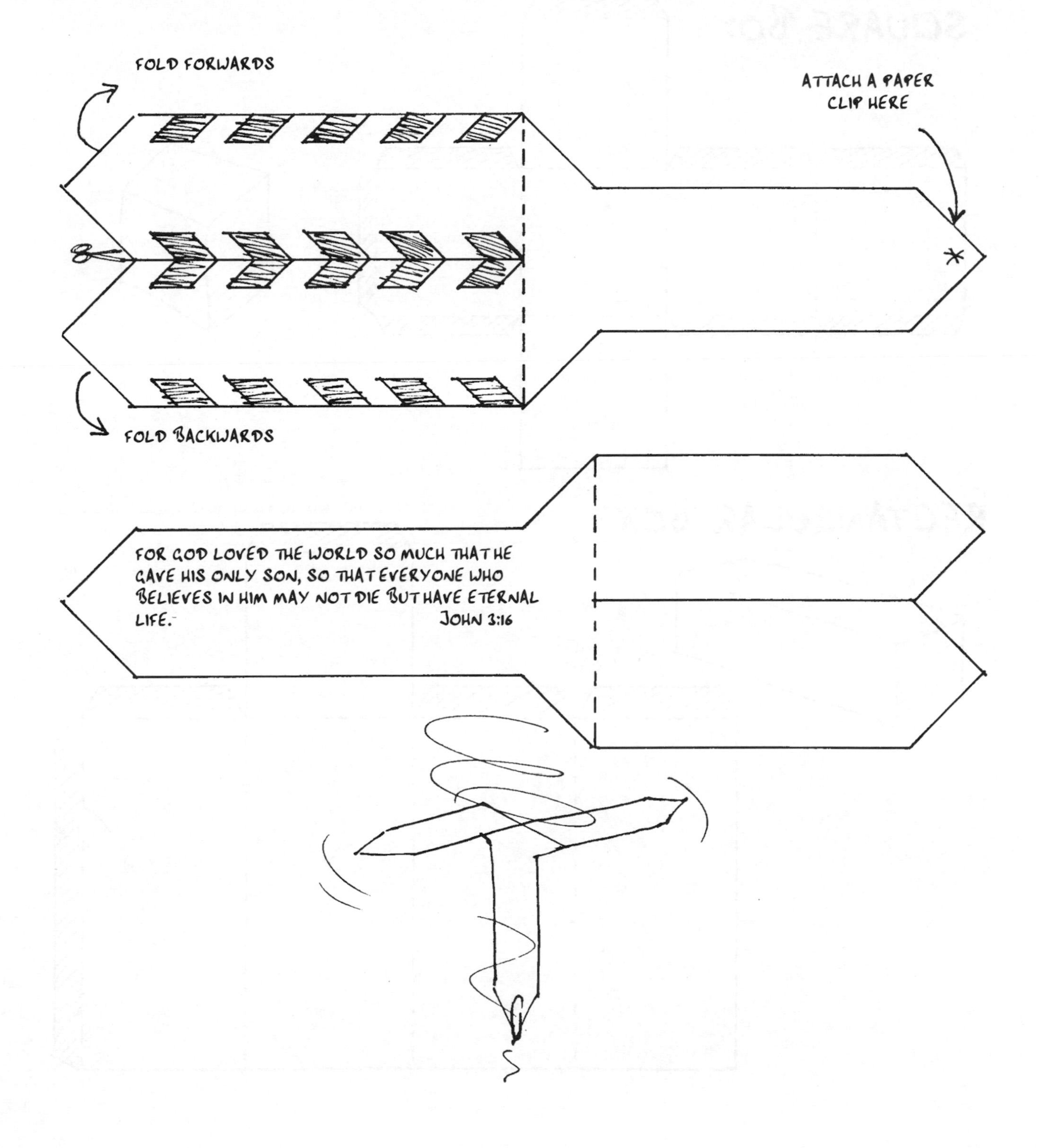

3 Boxes

Children love to make boxes and they can be used for so many different things – treasure boxes, money boxes, gift boxes, dice, boxes with a different memory verse written on each side, boxes with home-made sweets inside.

The two box patterns below will give you a square and a rectangular box. Photocopy the patterns onto thin card. Alternatively, use paper and paste the outline onto the back of a cereal packet or similar.

Don't forget that you can enlarge or reduce the pattern on a photocopier to achieve the size you need.

Box Patterns

Cut along the bold lines and fold along the dotted lines. Apply a little glue to the shaded tabs.

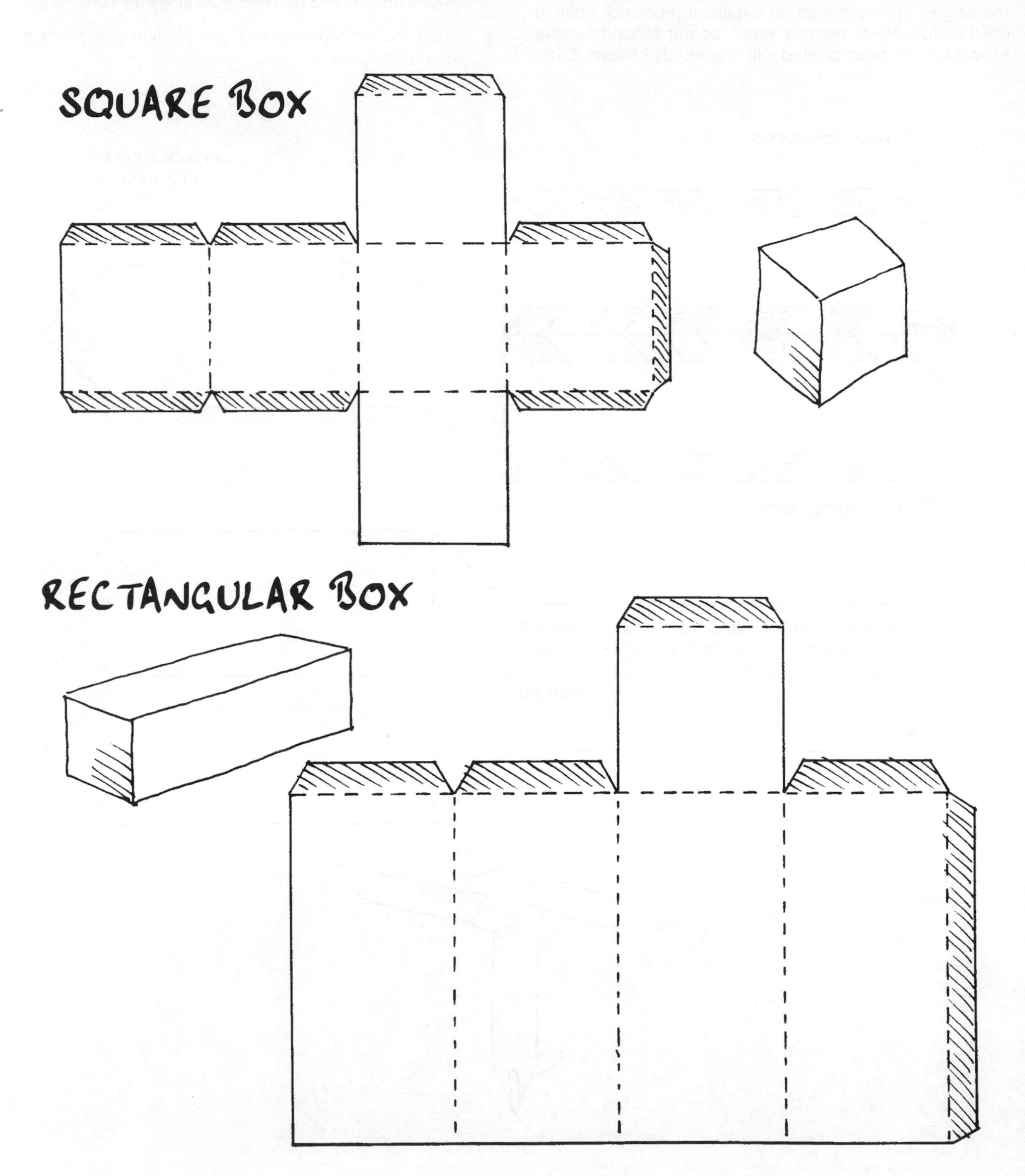

4 Fancy Fish

There are many fishing stories in the Bible, so you should have plenty of opportunities to make these simple but effective fish.

1. Cut out a simple fish shape.
2. Fold this in half lengthwise, and make angled cuts, longer in the middle and shorter on the outside.
3. Fold back each V-shaped cut.
4. Mount the fish on coloured paper, and add a caption. Alternatively, hang four or five of them from a covered coat-hanger to make a simple mobile.

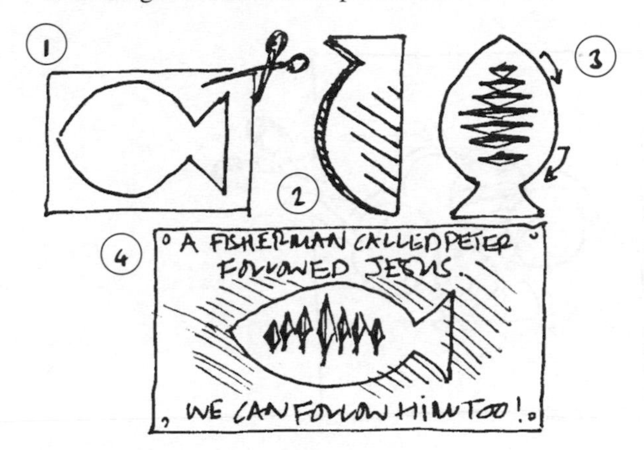

5 Concertina Birds

In the Old Testament, birds play an important role in the story of Noah; while in the New Testament, the Holy Spirit is likened to a dove: 'I saw the Spirit come down like a dove from heaven and stay on him' (John 1:32). To illustrate these, try making these simple concertina birds.

1. Cut out the shape of a bird's body from thin card. Draw an eye, and colour in the beak on both sides of the bird.
2. Take a rectangle of thin paper and pleat it, concertina-style.
3. Use a Stanley knife to cut a small slit in the side of each bird, round about where the wings should be. An adult should do this for each child. Push the pleated paper through the slit, and fan it out on either side, to make wings.
4. Pierce a small hole in the top of the bird and attach a piece of wool or thread. Tie the finished birds to a curtain pole and put it where they will catch the breeze.

6 Gobsmacked Message Cards!

These cards are particularly useful, since the speech bubble in the middle can be used in a hundred different ways! For example, you might use it to give details of a party, barbecue, outing, holiday club or other event. Alternatively, you could use the speech bubble to invite people to a family service, or to send a special message like 'Get well soon' or 'Congratulations!'

1. Take a piece of paper and a piece of card of exactly the same size. A5 works well. Fold them both in half and make a crease down the middle.
2. Cut a short slit near the middle of the fold in the paper.
3. Fold back the paper on either side of the slit, so that you have two triangular folds.
4. Very gently, tuck the triangles inside the folded paper.
5. Turn the paper over and glue it on to the card. Take care not to spread any glue on the beak/mouth.
6. When the glue is dry draw a picture on the inside and outside of the card to incorporate the beak/mouth in the centre.

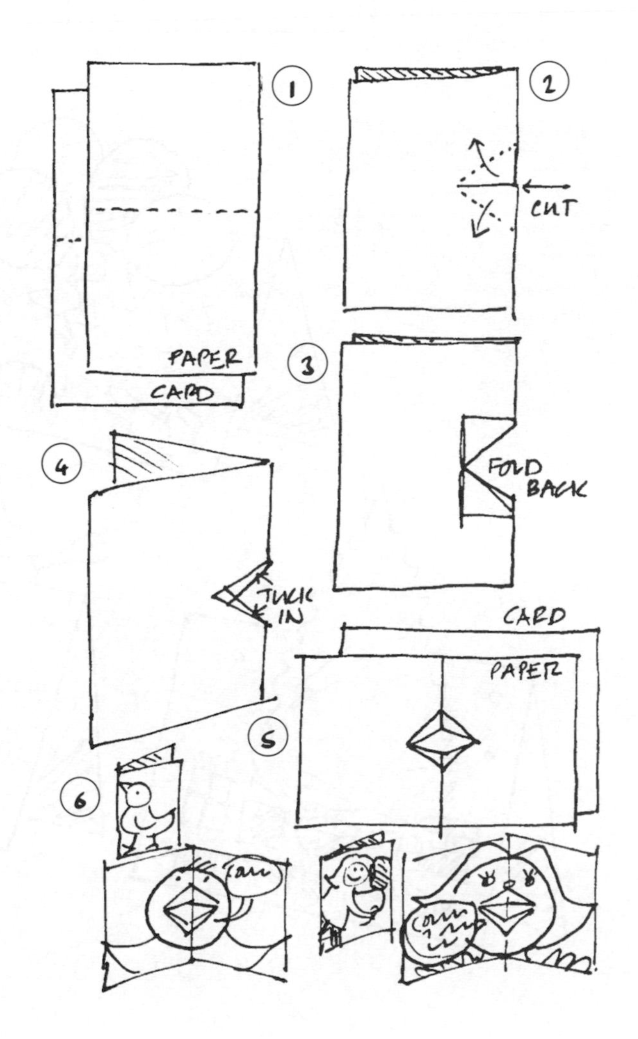

7 Stand-up Cards

Stand-up cards can be made in all shapes and sizes. Why not encourage the children to make a selection? Keep them in a safe place ready to send to members of your group or church when appropriate. It might be a good idea to prepare a number of welcome cards to give to newcomers. Inside each you could include details about the group: meeting times, term dates, relevant telephone numbers, and so on. Follow the instructions below to create your own stand-up cards.

For each you will need a rectangle of thin card (A5 works best), scissors and a packet of felt-tipped pens.

1. Take a rectangle of thin card and draw a simple picture on the front.
2. Carefully cut around the outline of the top half of the picture.
3. Then fold back the rest of the card and add a greeting at the bottom.
4. Use the same method to make a variety of different cards.

8 Christmas Tree Cards

Christmas tree cards look most effective if they can be made out of green paper or, even better, out of origami paper which has a second colour on the reverse. If this isn't possible, give the children sheets of A5 paper and let them colour each side a different colour.

Follow the instructions below to make your own 3D Christmas card.

1 Fold a piece of A5 paper in half.

2 Gently make a second fold down the middle of the front half of the card. Try not to crease this fold too firmly.

Very neatly, make five or six diagonal cuts, in this second fold. Make each cut slightly larger than the previous one.

Open out the front half of the card and fold down each V-shaped cut so that you have a mini-triangular flap. Use a ruler to help you make a straight fold. You should find that each flap is slightly larger than the previous one, which creates the appearance of a Christmas tree.

3 Draw a few lines to suggest hills in the background and add a few sticky-paper stars to the sky.

Help the children to write greetings and perhaps a Bible verse inside their cards. Provide envelopes so that they can send them to their friends.

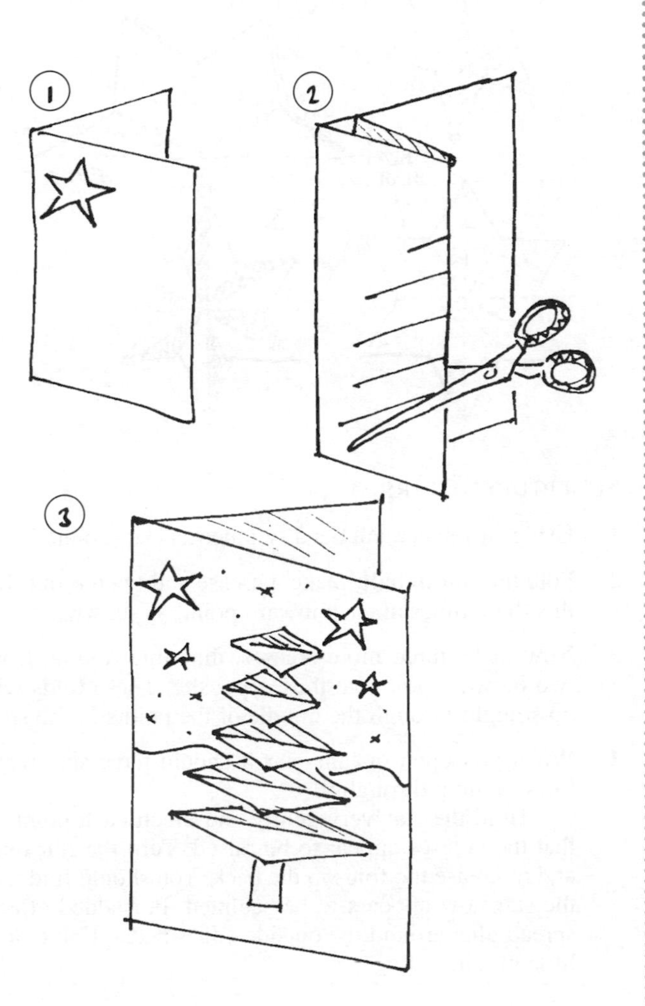

9 Quick Christmas Decorations

SIMPLE PAPER LANTERNS

1 Take an A4 piece of paper and colour it with a 'Christmassy' pattern. Alternatively, use a piece of Christmas gift wrap.

2 Cut off a strip about 1 inch or 25 mm wide along the bottom. Keep this to use as the handle.

3 Fold the rest of the paper in half horizontally, then make 8 or 10 cuts in the paper. Don't cut all the way to the edge.

4 Unfold the paper and fasten the ends together with sticky tape, as shown.

Finally, attach the handle with another piece of sticky tape, and the lantern is finished. Why not make a whole row of miniature lanterns to hang from a length of ribbon across your meeting room?

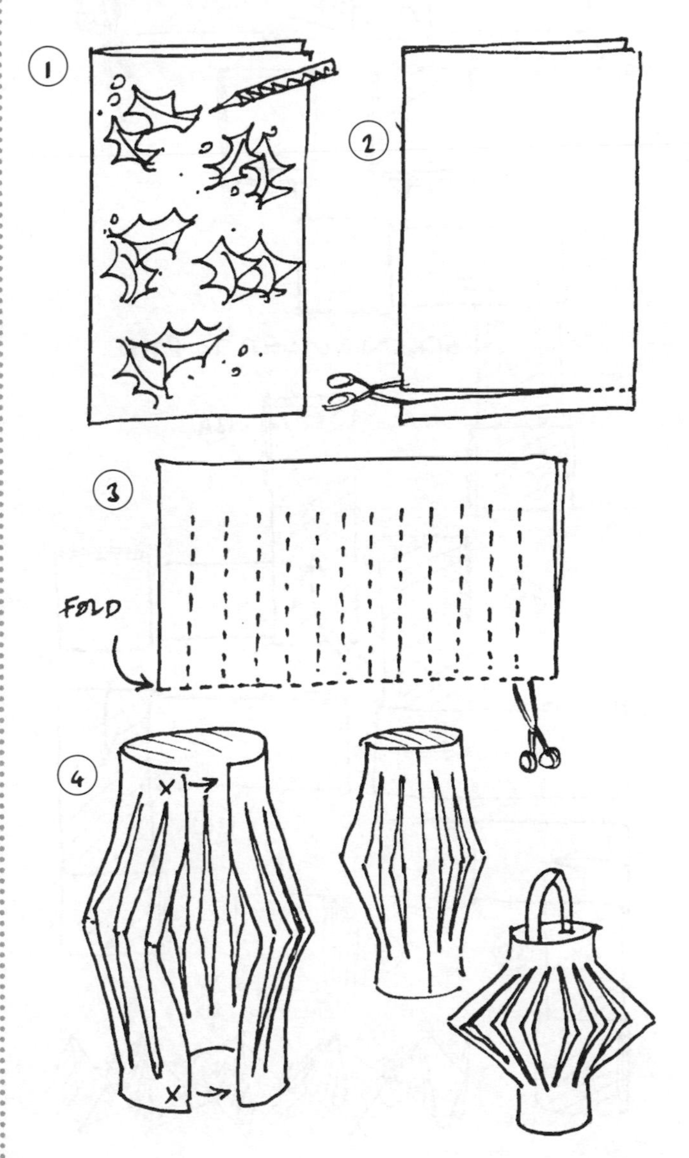

Paper Garland

1 Choose two different colours of crepe paper. Red and green work well at Christmas. Cut a 1.5 inch or 3.5 cm strip from the end of each roll of crepe paper.

2 Unroll the two colours a little way and then place the end of the red strip over the end of the green strip at right angles. Glue the two colours together at this point.

3 Now fold the green strip over the red strip and then fold the red strip back over the green strip. Continue in this way, making a sharp crease along each fold, until you reach the end of the crepe paper. Glue the last two folds together.

4 The finished garland can be draped around a Christmas tree, or hung across your meeting room.

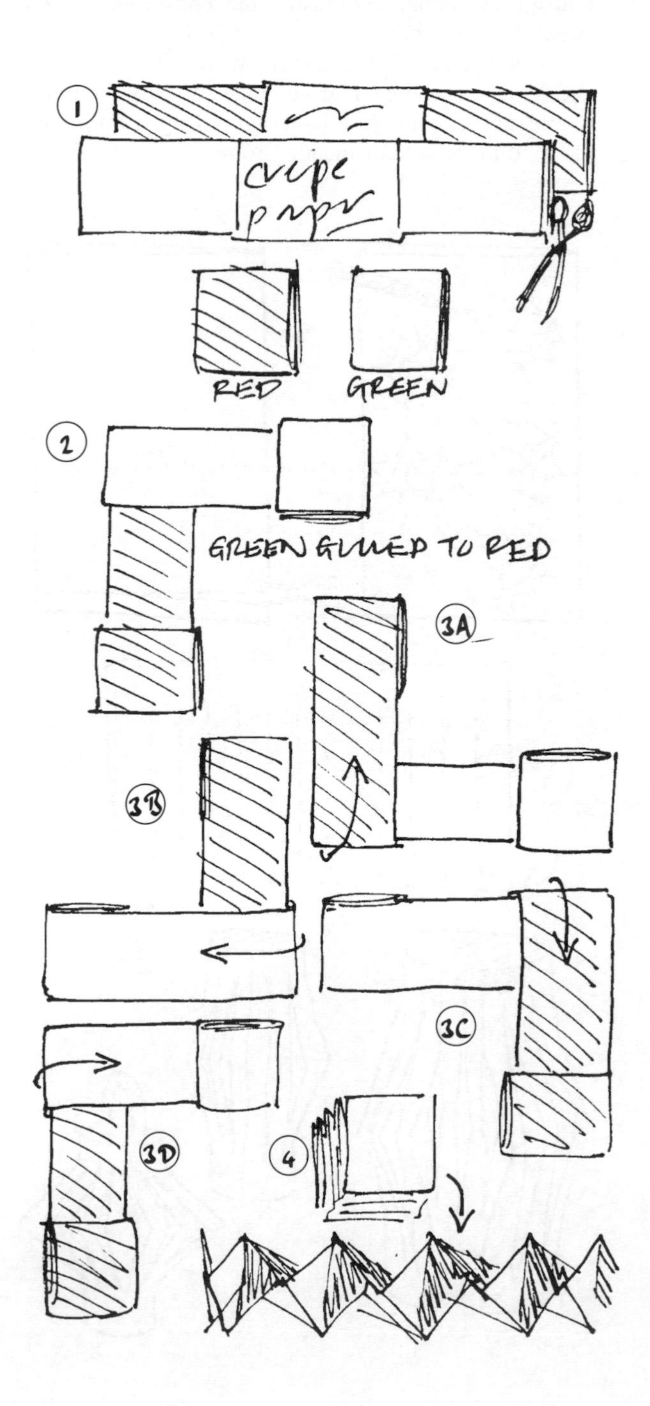

3D Stars

1 Cut out two identical stars from thin card or, even better, metallic card.

2 Mark a point in the centre of each star. Then make a slit in one star from the top down to the centre, and the other star from the bottom up to the centre.

3 Slot the two stars together until they meet in the centre.

4 Thread a needle with embroidery thread and push it through the two cut edges at the top of the star. Make a loop, and your star is ready to hang on the Christmas tree.

☞ Tip

A similar decoration can be made from a bell or Christmas tree shape, or indeed any symmetrical shape.

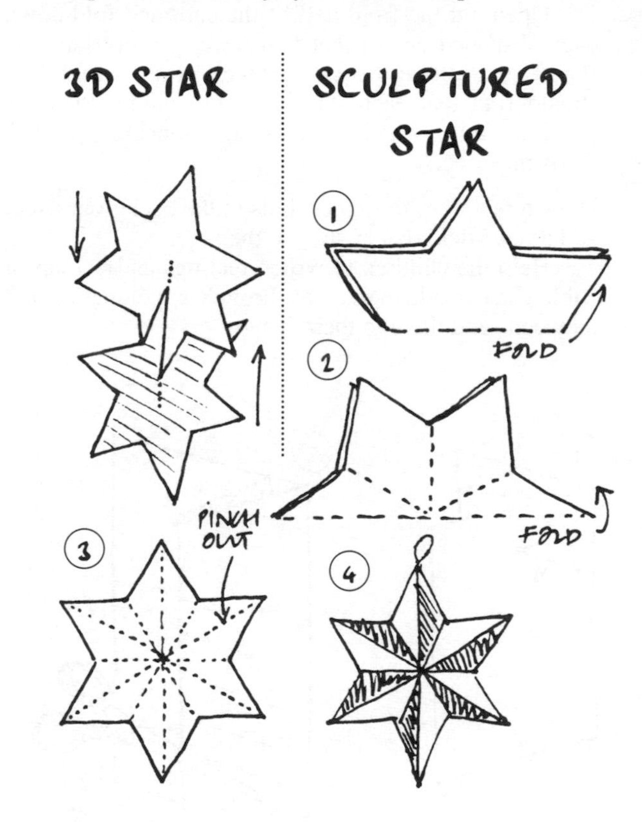

Sculptured stars

1 Using stiff paper, cut out a symmetrical six-pointed star.

2 Fold the star in half, make a crease and open it out. Do this three times at each inward point, as shown.

3 Now make three more creases, this time folding from two outward points to those opposite. These folds will go straight through the middle of the points of the star.

4 When you open out the star it should have six crease lines running through it.

Hold the star very gently and pinch each point so that the creases appear to be raised. Turn the star over and re-crease the folds in the back. You should find that the star now appears to be sculpted. For added effect, spread glue around the outside edges and sprinkle on a little glitter.

10 Link-up Frieze

A linked frieze makes a simple but effective display. Enlarge the artwork on a photocopier to the size you require. Give each child one shape to colour or decorate with sticky shapes, then link all the shapes together to make a frieze. The linked shapes can be used in several ways. Here are just three ideas.

1 At the beginning of a year you might want to make a frieze as a way of getting to know the children. Give each child a shape and ask them to write their name in decorative writing, plus one thing they like and one thing they dislike.

2 On another occasion you could use the shapes as a way of learning the memory verse. Write each word of the verse on a separate shape in outline lettering and ask the children to colour in the words to make a memory-verse frieze.

3 You could use the shapes as a way of scoring for a quiz. Award an elephant or monkey for each correct answer. The team with the longest trail of elephants or chain of monkeys wins.

5 Ten ways to learn a memory verse

A WORD ABOUT MEMORY VERSES

If you went to a traditional Sunday School as a child, you probably know all about memory verses, or 'golden texts'. You may even still remember some of the verses you learnt as a child. Since children can retain things more easily than adults, it's an excellent idea to teach them a selection of key Bible verses which will, hopefully, stay with them for life. It's almost impossible to learn a new verse every week, but a verse each month or a verse for each series is a realistic target.

When we teach a memory verse it's important that the children understand what we believe about these words of scripture. They are more than just words we like or words from a storybook. Memory verses are words from the Bible, and, since Christians believe the Bible is inspired by God, they are words with a special importance.

CHOOSING THE RIGHT VERSE

Choosing a suitable memory verse to match a particular Bible story is no easy task! It's tempting to choose a verse directly from the story. However, this isn't always the best route to take. Let's look at the story of the storm on the lake. If we choose a verse from that story, we might end up with:

> Jesus got up and gave an order to the wind and the stormy water; they died down, and there was a great calm. *(Luke 8:24)*

However, if we select a verse from elsewhere in the Bible, we can choose something that speaks more directly to the children. Begin by taking a second look at your aim for the session. Perhaps you have decided to tell the story of the storm on the lake to help the children understand that just as Jesus was there for the disciples when they were afraid and needed him, so we know he is always there for us. In which case a more suitable verse might be:

> The Lord is with me, I will not be afraid… *(Psalm 118:6)*

Alternatively, your aim might be to show how Jesus is all-powerful, the Lord of all nature. In which case you might choose the following verse:

> The Lord rules supreme in heaven, greater than the roar of the ocean, more powerful than the waves of the sea. *(Psalm 93:4)*

As far as possible, it's important to choose memory verses which may prove useful to the children in later life, verses which will:

- Help them worship God
- Give reassurance in times of worry, or guidance in times of difficulty
- Teach something about God – Father, Son and Holy Spirit
- Serve as a reminder of the beliefs at the heart of the Christian faith.

Here is a selection of verses you might find useful. They have been chosen to fit in with key festivals in the Christian calendar. The wording has been taken from the *Good News Bible*.

- *Christmas:*
  '…he will be called Immanuel' (which means 'God is with us'). *(Matthew 1:23)*

  God showed his love for us by sending his only Son into the world, so that we might have life through him. *(1 John 4:9)*

- *Easter:*
  'For God loved the world so much that he gave his only Son, so that everyone who believes in him may not die but have eternal life.' *(John 3:16)*

  We believe that Jesus died and rose again… *(1 Thessalonians 4:14)*

- *Pentecost:*
  For the Spirit that God has given us does not make us timid; instead, his Spirit fills us with power, love, and self-control. *(2 Timothy 1:7)*

- *Harvest:*
  What a rich harvest your goodness provides! *(Psalm 65:11)*

  The land has produced its harvest; God, our God, has blessed us. *(Psalm 67:6)*

  He gives food to every living creature; his love is eternal. *(Psalm 136:25)*

- *New Year:*
  Jesus Christ is the same yesterday, today, and for ever. *(Hebrews 13:8)*

- *Bible Sunday:*
  Your word is a lamp to guide me and a light for my path. *(Psalm 119:105)*

  All Scripture is inspired by God… *(2 Timothy 3:16)*

- *Church Anniversary:*
  I remember the days gone by; I think about all that you have done, I bring to mind all your deeds. *(Psalm 143:5)*

In section 2, ten Bible stories are used as examples of different methods of telling a story. If you decide to use some of these stories with your group, you may also like to consider the following memory verses:

1 *The shepherds hear about the birth of Jesus:*
'This very day in David's town your Saviour was born – Christ the Lord!' *(Luke 2:11)*

2 *The two house builders:*
'So then, anyone who hears these words of mine and obeys them is like a wise man who built his house on rock.' *(Matthew 7:24)*

3 *The storm on the lake:*
The Lord rules supreme in heaven,
greater than the roar of the ocean,
more powerful than the waves of the sea
(Psalm 93:4)

The Lord is with me, I will not be afraid…
(Psalm 118:6)

4 *The parable of the lost sheep:*
'I am the good shepherd. As the Father knows me and I know the Father, in the same way I know my sheep and they know me. And I am willing to die for them.' *(John 10:14–15)*

…how broad and long, how high and deep, is Christ's love. *(Ephesians 3:18)*

5 *Jesus visits Mary and Martha:*
Be still, and know that I am God…
(Psalm 46:10, NIV)

Come near to God, and he will come near to you.
(James 4:8)

6 *Zacchaeus:*
Anyone who is joined to Christ is a new being;
the old is gone, the new has come.
(2 Corinthians 5:17)

7 *The parable of the good Samaritan:*
'My commandment is this: love one another, just as I love you.' *(John 15:12)*

8 *Jesus and Peter walk on water:*
I look to the Lord for help at all times
and he rescues me from danger.
(Psalm 25:15)

9 *Doubting Thomas:*
We believe that Jesus died and rose again…
(1 Thessalonians 4:4)

' How happy are those who believe without seeing me! *(John 20:29)*

10 *Blind Bartimaeus:*
I will praise you, Lord, with all my heart;
I will tell of all the wonderful things you have done. *(Psalm 9:1)*

1 Balloon Verse

Use a thick marker pen to write each word, including the Bible reference, of your chosen memory verse on a separate balloon. A black or blue pen on yellow or orange balloons shows up the most clearly. Give each balloon to a member of the group and ask those with balloons to come and stand at the front. The rest of the group must then tell those at the front where to stand so that the words on the balloons can be read in the correct order. Read the verse out loud over and over again to help the children commit the words to memory. After each time, pop one of the balloons so that the children have to fill in the gaps from memory. By the end the whole group should be able to recite the verse without any help.

Alternatively, write the words of the memory verse on individual slips of paper, fold up each slip and put it inside a balloon before you blow it up. The children must burst all the balloons, retrieve the slips of paper and lay out the words of the memory verse in the correct order. If you have a large number of children, you could make this a team activity with a set of balloons for each team. The first team to complete the task wins. If the children have not yet heard the memory verse, you may need to supply each team with a Bible to help them reconstruct the verse.

☞ TIP
Put the balloons in a large black plastic bin-bag until you want to use them; otherwise they might burst before you're ready!

2 Washing-line

Using a marker pen, write each word of the verse on a separate sheet of A4 paper. Tie a length of string or washing-line across one end of your meeting room and have enough clothes pegs ready to attach the words to the line. You now have three possible ways to use your washing-line.

- Give the children the words and ask them to use the clothes pegs to attach them to the washing-line in the right order.
- Peg all the words on the washing-line in the wrong order and ask the children to rearrange them so that the memory verse is correct.
- Peg every other word on the washing-line and ask the children to fill in the gaps.

If you are using this memory verse for a series, you might like to use one of these ideas each week.

Once the memory verse has been pegged out correctly, read out the verse three or four times, each time taking down some of the words so that the children end up reciting the verse from memory.

3 Wall of Words

Take a sheet of A4 paper for each word in your verse. Use scissors to slightly round off the edges, so that the sheets of paper look like rustic brick shapes! Write one word on each brick shape and, using *Blu-tack*, ask the children to fix them to the wall in two or three rows to look like a wall. Repeat the verse over and over again, removing one or two bricks each time, until the group knows the verse by heart.

When the children return the following week, have all the words fixed to the wall in the right order but back to front. Revise the verse by picking bricks at random and asking the children if they can tell you which word is on the other side. Turn the word over if they answer correctly. Continue until the whole verse has been reconstructed.

4 Wallpaper Border

Wallpaper borders are all the fashion these days, so why not turn some of your memory verses into a long thin border to be fixed around the top of the wall in your meeting room? Cut a long thin strip of paper, a piece cut from the back of an old roll of wallpaper will work well. Write out the words in outline lettering so that the children can decorate or colour in the words. Have ready a selection of felt-tipped pens, sticky shapes, glitter, and so on. If you have a large number of children, you could cut the verse into sections and let them work in small groups on just two or three words.

☞ TIP
Some people have a special PC sign-writing software package. If you ask around, you may find someone who can print the verse in outline lettering for you.

5 Fishing Game

Make your own magnetic fishing game! First, make a fishing rod by tying a length of string to one end of a garden cane and attaching a magnet to the other end. Then cut out at least one paper fish-shape for each word in your memory verse. You might like to use the fish template on p 61. Write one word of the verse on each fish, and fix a paper-clip to each one. Put all the fish in a bucket and let the children 'fish' for the words one by one, using the magnetic rod.

If you only have a small group, make a rod and a set of fish for each child. Cut each set of fish out of different coloured pieces of paper so that each child is fishing for his own colour. If you want the game to last longer, number the backs of the fish and insist that the words must be fished out in the right order, otherwise the fish must be thrown back!

If you have a large group, divide the children into teams and have a set of fish, a bucket and a rod for each team. Ask the teams to line up at one end of the room and place a bucket at the other end. Each member of the team must race up to her bucket, pull out a fish and return to her team. The first team to complete the verse, learn it and recite it from memory, wins.

☞ TIP
Keep all the 'fishing tackle' in a safe place so that you can use it again. Next time you might like to write the words on octopus-shapes, or shark- and seaweed-shapes, with one or two old boots thrown in for good measure!

6 Coded Verses

Children love to get their teeth into a really tricky code. If you have a computer, you should be able to create a 'symbol' code, eg A=✻, B=❄, C=✱ ', etc. Or you could run the alphabet backwards, eg 'A=Z, B=Y, C=X', etc. Young children enjoy finding a verse that has been hidden amongst a selection of extra letters, eg 'XYGOZYDZZISX YYLOZXXVXE'.

Don't feel you have to write the whole verse in code. With younger children it's often enough just to exchange all the vowels for something different. Or pick out three or four of the most common letters and swap them for something else – a picture or number perhaps (see the example opposite).

You may also like to try a team challenge. Divide the children into groups and give each group a verse and a code to write it in. After a few minutes, all the groups exchange their coded verses plus the codebreakers, and each group then deciphers another group's work.

7 Jigsaw

Try turning the memory verse into a jigsaw puzzle. Write out the words on a large sheet of paper or thin card, then cut it up to make a puzzle. Cut it into thirty or so small pieces for older children, but only into ten or fifteen larger pieces for younger ones. Either give the children all the pieces in an envelope, or hide them around your meeting room so that they have to find all the pieces in order to complete the puzzle.

If you want to turn the activity into a team game, use different coloured sheets of paper for the puzzles and get each team to look for a particular colour.

A jigsaw puzzle need not always be rectangular. You may like to try a circular, triangular or square puzzle. If you are looking at the parable of the lost sheep, why not have a sheep-shaped puzzle?

8 Making Music

Why not turn the memory verse into a song? Choose a well-known tune that all the group will know, perhaps a favourite TV theme tune or a popular song like 'Frère Jacques' or the Skye Boat Song. Then try to make the words fit the music. You may need to repeat some words or to slightly rephrase them in modern English, but you will find that it's an excellent way of learning and remembering the message of the verse. Even if you don't finish with a chart-topping song, the effort of setting the words to music will fix the verse in the children's memories.

Try singing Psalm 46:1 to the tune 'Frère Jacques':

God's our shelter,
    God's our shelter
And our strength,
    And our strength.
Always there to help us,
    Always there to help us.
When there's trouble,
    When there's trouble.

Picture alphabet code

Just for fun, try out the following code. You will find the answer at the bottom of the page, but you shouldn't need it

9 Spinners and Spirals

Memory Verse Spinners

1. Cut a circle about 10 cm in diameter out of thick card. Alternatively, use two circles cut from a cornflakes packet and pasted together.
2. Decorate the circle on both sides with a bright and colourful design and write the words of the memory verse on one side.
3. Make two small holes in the centre of the circle, approximately 2 cm apart. Thread a length of thin string or embroidery thread (approx 60 cm) through the holes and tie the ends together to make a loop.
4. To make the spinner whizz around, hold the end loops of the thread around your index fingers and twirl the spinner so that the thread becomes twisted. Then pull the thread taut and watch the spinner unwind at speed.

☞ Tip

You'll find that spinners work best when the card is fairly heavy.

Memory Verse Spirals

Once again, cut a circle of card, but this time draw a line that creates spiral inside the circle, getting smaller and smaller until it reaches the middle. The words of the memory verse can be written in decorative writing along this line. Cut along the line so that you have a coil of card. Then thread a needle with some coloured cotton, push it through the centre of the card and tie off the thread. Gently pull out the cardboard so that it hangs down in a spiral. Tie the cotton to a curtain pole above a radiator, and watch the spiral spin around as the warm air rises.

10 Bookmarks

Bookmarks can be made in many different shapes, and even if the children aren't keen on reading they can still make a bookmark as a present or use it to mark the relevant story in their Bible. Try to choose a shape that fits in with the verse or Bible story. Thus a verse about Christmas could have a star shape at the top of the bookmark; a verse about Jesus the Good Shepherd could fit with a sheep-shaped bookmark; and a verse about God's special love for every person might suit a simple gingerbread-man outline. Whatever shape you choose, punch a hole in the top of your bookmark and add a strand of wool to make a tassel.

☞ Tip

You might find that some of the templates on pp 60–63 can be turned into bookmarks.

✖ Cross Reference

It's also worth checking out section 4:2 'Helicopters'; section 4:3 'Boxes'; section 4:10 'Link-up Frieze'.

Answer to Picture Alphabet code

'We know that there is only the one God', 1 Corinthians 8:4.

6 Ten mini-sports

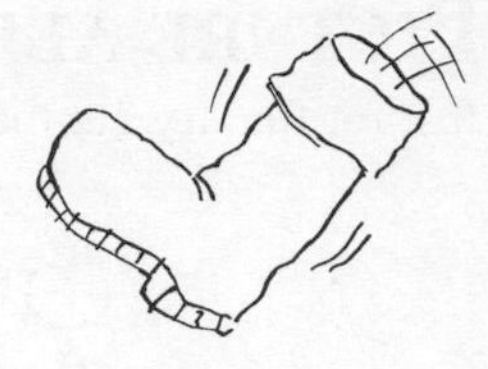

If you have a large group of children and about an hour to fill, then mini-sports – or potted-sports as it is sometimes called – are a wonderful way of keeping everyone involved and occupied. Set up a number of activities all around your meeting room, and put one leader or an older child in charge of each one. Try to have a variety that will appeal to all tastes and skills. Choose some activities that require physical fitness, some that require manual dexterity and some that rely on a lucky break. You could even put in a quiet game to challenge the children's brain cells, eg 'Find a Square'.

Explain to the children that you want them to have a go at everything, but they can choose which activity they try first. Make sure they understand that there is a fixed time-limit to try as many activities as possible. Point out that it makes sense not to waste time waiting at the end of a long queue since they can always return when the queue is shorter.

Give each child a card with his or her name on and a list of the activities. If you are organising a mini-sports event to raise money for charity, you could charge the children a nominal sum for their game cards. They should take their cards to the leader in charge of each activity and ask him or her to mark their scores in the appropriate box. If you have plenty of time, allow the children to return to an activity for a second or third attempt once they have completed all the others. This will keep the speedy children busy while the slower children are still trying to decide which queue to join!

MINI-SPORTS SCORE CARD

NAME ....

GAME	1ST TRY	2ND TRY	3RD TRY	BEST SCORE
WELLY WANGING				
SKIPPING				
SLOW BICYCLE				
SKITTLES				
PEG GAME				
GOAL SHOOTING				
WET SPONG RACE				
CHOPSTICK CHALLENGE				

If you only have two or three leaders, ask each leader to organise two or more games. Have an interval for refreshments half way through the event. This will give the leaders a chance to put away one game and set up another.

At the end, add up the scores and award small prizes for the best score in each event and the best overall score in each age-group. Alternatively, you could make medals out of chocolate money attached to a length of ribbon. It will help the leader who is in charge of adding up the scores if everyone agrees on a simple, standard scoring system.

☞ TIP

A mini-sports event makes an excellent all-age activity.

1 Peg Game

Tie a length of washing-line between two chairs and attach ten or more pegs to it. Challenge the children to see how many pegs they can remove from the line and hold in one hand only. The other hand should be tucked behind the back. Score one point for every peg removed. You may like to give younger children two points for each peg.

2 Slow Bike Race

Bring in a bicycle and section off one side of your meeting room or, even better, take the bike outside. Explain to the children that the aim is to cycle from one end of the hall to the other as slowly as possible, while you time them with a stopwatch. This will test their ability to balance on a bicycle. Try out this challenge beforehand and decide how you will award points. Perhaps the children could score one point for every two seconds they take.

3 Exercise Bike Challenge

If you are able to bring in an exercise bike with a speedometer which registers the distance covered, challenge the children to cycle a mile or a kilometre in a fixed time-limit, eg 60 seconds. Award points according to how close they come to the target time.

4 Skipping

Challenge the children to discover how many consecutive skips they can manage in two minutes. Allow younger children to restart and continue counting if they make a mistake, but insist that older children start again. Award one point for every ten skips.

5 Darts

If you can find a set of Velcro or suction darts, use these to set up a simple game. Allow older children just three throws and younger children more according to their age. Set a target of 180 to score the maximum ten points.

6 Skittles

Set up a skittle game in one corner of your meeting room. If you don't have a proper set of skittles, you could try ten plastic drink bottles weighted with a little sand or water, or even ten empty cans. Allow the children three throws to knock over all ten skittles, and score one point for every skittle that falls. Younger children could be given an extra throw to even up the competition.

7 Two Football Games

Dribble a Football

Set up a short slalom using cones or similar markers. Ask the children to dribble a football around the course. Start with 10 points and knock off points if they hit a cone or take too long to complete the course.

Goal Hole

Cut a large hole in a huge piece of card, or use a hoop wedged between two chairs as a goal mouth. Draw a chalk line on the floor at a distance from the 'goal'. Give the children five attempts at shooting a football into the hole from the chalk line. Score 2 points for each successful goal.

8 Welly Wanging

Organise a competition to see how far each child can throw a Wellington boot. For obvious reasons this is a game that works best outside! Give older children a large man's welly boot and younger children a smaller lady's one. Measure each child's throw with a tape measure and award 10 points to all those who throw beyond a certain distance. Allocate the remaining points for shorter throws in proportion to the distance thrown.

9 Three Transfer Tests

Peas Please!

Set out two bowls side by side, one empty bowl and one filled with dried peas. Give the children a straw each and one minute to transfer as many peas into the empty bowl as they can manage. They will have to transfer the peas one by one, sucking them onto the end of their straws. Set a target number to achieve the maximum 10 points.

Wet Sponge Race

This game works best if you are able to go outside. Place two buckets about ten feet apart; one should be empty and the other full of water. Give the children a large bath sponge and a fixed time-limit to transfer as much water from one bucket to the other as they possibly can. At the end of that time, measure the level of water with a ruler and award points accordingly.

Chopstick Challenge

Place two bowls side by side, one should be empty and the other full of uncooked pasta shapes. Challenge the children to transfer as many pasta shapes as they can from one bowl to the other, using a pair of chopsticks. Insist that they only use one hand and have the other hand tucked behind their back. At the end of the time-limit, count out the pasta shapes and award points accordingly.

10 Find a Square

On a photocopier, enlarge and make several copies of the square on p 42 on coloured paper. Cut out the pieces and tuck them into an envelope. If you have a large group of children, you may like to cut out two or three sets, so that more than one child can attempt this challenge at any one time. Give the children the envelope and ask them to put the pieces together to make a square. Award 10 points to any child who completes the task in under 60 seconds, 8 points to children who take less than 90 seconds, 6 points to those who take less than 2 minutes, and so on.

FIND A SQUARE

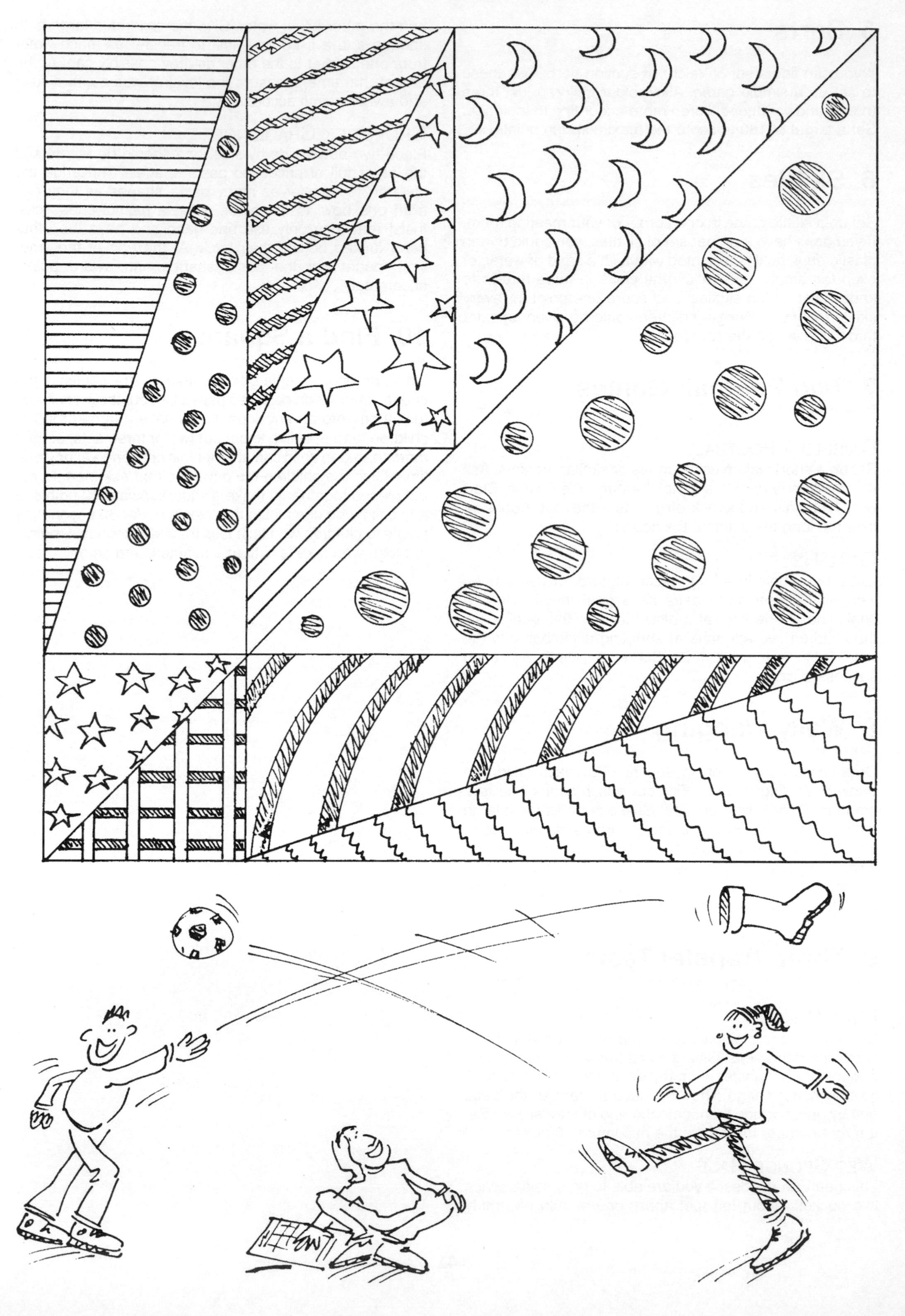

7 Ten examples of easy experiments

The world is a wonderful place, and was created by our amazing God. Children love to watch experiments and to understand how everyday things act and react. The following easy experiments have been chosen, partly because they are simple and you will find everything you need at home, but more importantly because they can be used to teach us something special about God.

PRACTISE MAKES PERFECT!

It's always a good idea to practise experiments in advance, to get the hang of the materials and the instructions before going public! It's also a good idea to time each stage of the experiment and to check that you can achieve the desired end result. After all, you don't want to disappoint your audience.

1 Hovering Table-tennis Ball

For this experiment you will need a powerful hairdryer and a table-tennis ball. Switch the hairdryer on to full power and place a table-tennis ball in the current of air. You will find that the hairdryer keeps the ball suspended in the air, and when the hairdryer is moved the ball moves with it. Try raising and lowering the hairdryer, moving it from side to side and tilting it. Wherever the hairdryer goes, the ball goes too. The hairdryer supports the ball and gives it 'life'. The ball is totally dependent on the power of the hairdryer: without it, the ball would fall to the ground and soon run out of 'bounce'. Use this experiment as an illustration of our dependence on God. You may like to base your comments on one of the following verses:

> I depend on God alone;
> I put my hope in him. *(Psalm 62:5)*

> Let us keep our eyes fixed on Jesus, on whom our faith depends from beginning to end.
> *(Hebrews 12:2)*

☞ TIP

If your hairdryer doesn't support a table-tennis ball, you need to borrow a more powerful hairdryer from a friend!

2 Two Experiments with Ink-stained Flowers

BLUE DAFFODILS

Did you know that if you put a generous dose of blue ink into a vase of daffodils or white carnations, the flowers will gradually turn blue? The general effect is very strange!

Make the point to your group that a blue daffodil looks quite wrong. It isn't the beautiful flower God intended it to be – it has been contaminated by the blue ink. Use this experiment with older children as a way in to discussing how people sometimes allow things like horoscopes, lucky charms, tarot cards, Ouija boards, abuse of drugs, alcohol and nicotine to contaminate their lives. All these things can seriously spoil our lives and our relationship with God. But God wants to give us the chance to make a fresh start, and if we give our lives to him and ask him to forgive us, then all the stains and all the wrongdoing will be washed away.

You may like to include the following verses in your talk:

> So then, let us purify ourselves from everything that makes body or soul unclean, and let us be completely holy by living in awe of God.
> *(2 Corinthians 7:1)*

> If we confess our sins to God, he will keep his promise and do what is right: he will forgive us our sins and purify us from all our wrongdoing. *(1 John 1:9)*

☞ TIP

With younger children, the same experiment can be used to talk about how greed, selfishness, unkind behaviour, cheating, and so on, can spoil our lives.

HALF AND HALF

To achieve an even more curious effect, cut the lower two-thirds of the stem of a carnation in half lengthwise with a sharp knife. Then position the flower so that one half of the stem is in a glass of clear water and the other half in a glass of ink and water. Over a period of two or three days, you will find that half the flower takes on a 'bluish' colour, while the other half remains white.

Point out that a flower which is half blue and half white doesn't look natural: it's neither one colour nor the other. Something is quite evidently wrong. In the same way it's impossible to be half a Christian. If we love God, we should love him with all our hearts, all our minds and all our bodies, seven days a week, twenty-four hours a day.

> 'Love the Lord your God with all your heart, with all your soul, and with all your mind.'
> *(Matthew 22:37)*

3 Rainbow Promises

Make a rainbow to remind children of the promise God made to Noah. You will need a mirror, a lump of plasticine, a powerful torch, a shallow dish (eg a lasagne dish) and a sheet of white paper. Fill the dish three-quarters full with water. Then position the mirror in the dish so that it slopes backwards; use the plasticine to fix it in place. Switch the torch on and shine the light on the part of the mirror that is under the water. Hold the sheet of paper at an angle above the torch and you should find that a rainbow appears. If you don't succeed the first time, try tilting the torch at different angles or darkening your room.

Explain to the children that just as God made this promise to Noah, so he has made a special promise to everyone who believes in him. He has promised the gift of eternal life to all those who ask forgiveness for their wrongdoing and give their life to Jesus.

> 'Whenever I cover the sky with clouds and the rainbow appears, I will remember my promise to you and to all the animals that a flood will never again destroy all living beings.' *(Genesis 9:14–15)*

> 'For God loved the world so much that he gave his only Son, so that everyone who believes in him may not die but have eternal life.' *(John 3:16)*

> The Lord is faithful to his promises... *(Psalm 145:13)*

4 Washed Clean

For this experiment you will need an old white handkerchief and a water-soluble overhead projector pen. You will also need a bowl of very hot soapy water.

Explain to the children that all the things we do wrong make us dirty on the inside. Ask them for some suggestions of things that can spoil our lives, eg hate, anger, greed, envy, impatience, prejudice. Younger children will probably suggest concrete examples like telling lies, fighting with a brother/sister, being naughty, taking things that don't belong to you. Using a water-soluble overhead projector pen, write all these words or phrases on the handkerchief.

Explain to the children that Jesus wants to give each of us a fresh, clean start. When we ask him, he is always ready to forgive our wrongdoing. Take the handkerchief that has been spoilt by all the bad qualities and wash it in the bowl of hot soapy water. All the bad things are washed away and the handkerchief comes out clean. This is just how it is with our lives when we ask Jesus to forgive us – we are completely washed clean.

> 'You are stained red with sin, but I will wash you as clean as snow. Although your stains are deep red, you will be as white as wool.' *(Isaiah 1:18)*

☞ TIP

If you find that the ink doesn't wash out completely, either use a biological soap powder, or add a drop of bleach to the water. But if you do this, don't forget to wear rubber gloves, and don't let the children touch the water.

If you want to take this experiment one step further, ask the children to suggest some of the good and bad qualities that are part of all our lives. Write the good qualities (eg love, joy, peace, patience, kindness, generosity) in permanent ink, and write the bad qualities in water-soluble ink. Then, when you wash the handkerchief, you will find that only the bad qualities are washed away and the good ones remain!

5 All Equal, All Valued

Begin by making the point that God loves everyone equally. He created each one of us and loves us just as we are. Whether we have grey, green, blue or brown eyes; whether we have auburn, dark or fair hair; whether we are tall or short; whatever the colour of our skin, God loves us completely and he couldn't possibly love us any more than he does. God is without prejudice and takes no notice of our outward appearance.

Take a tube of Smarties and put a sweet of each colour into a glass of water. Watch as the colours dissolve in the water and you are left with a handful of sweets that are all white on the outside and chocolate brown in the middle. They are all identical and all equal. God treats each believer on the same basis; black or white, rich or poor, young or old, we are all equally precious to God.

> Peter began to speak: 'I now realise that it is true that God treats everyone on the same basis. Those who worship him and do what is right are acceptable to him, no matter what race they belong to.' *(Acts 10:34–35)*

6 Don't Hide Your Light!

You may remember this experiment from your own days at school! You will need a heat-proof bowl, a candle holder and a candle, a mirror and a box of matches. Explain to your group that God wants Christians to be like a light for the whole world: a light that helps people to see the right way (a torch), a light that shines in the darkness (a street lamp), a light that illuminates all that is good in the world (a spotlight), a light that warns people of danger (a lighthouse), a light that sheds a warm glow (a lamp).

> [Jesus said] 'No one lights a lamp and puts it under a bowl; instead he puts it on the lampstand, where it gives light for everyone in the house.' *(Matthew 5:15)*

Light your candle and put a bowl over the top. At first you can no longer see the light, but then after a few moments, when you remove the bowl, you will find that the candle has burnt up all the oxygen and the flame has gone out. (If you want the group to watch the flame go out, repeat the experiment with a glass bowl.) Explain to the children that a lamp hidden under a bowl is useless. Equally, Christians who hide their love for God and keep their faith a secret are also useless.

Light the candle a second time and this time put a mirror behind it. You should find that the light is twice as bright. If Christians are to be effective in the world, they must reflect God's love to others just as the mirror reflects the light of the candle.

7 Electric Balloon

Blow up a balloon and tie a knot in the end. Spend a few moments rubbing the balloon hard against your sweater. The experiment only works if the sweater is made of wool. The balloon will now be charged with static electricity and have the power to pick up very light things. Scatter a spoonful of sugar on a table and hold the balloon just above it. You should find that some of the sugar sticks to the outside of the balloon. Tear some paper into very small pieces, and scatter those on the table and you will find that the same thing happens.

Just as the electric balloon attracts or draws the sugar and paper, so God wants Christians to draw others to him. As Christians there should be something different and special about us, something that will make others stop and realise they are missing something important. Jesus told his disciples that if they really loved each other, other people would realise they were his followers.

> 'If you have love for one another, then everyone
> will know that you are my disciples.
> *(John 13:35)*

If Christians show love for each other, it will rub off on others. They will attract more people to follow Jesus, just like the balloon attracted the sugar.

8 Strength in Numbers

Have you ever heard someone say that they can't see the need to go to church because they can just as easily be a Christian at home? Besides the fact that it's important to go to church to give God the worship he deserves, it's also essential for us as Christians to be supported by the fellowship of other believers.

Invite a volunteer to come out to the front, then ask her if she feels strong enough to tear up a sheet of paper. Of course, that won't be difficult, but get her to do it all the same! Then give your volunteer a telephone directory and ask her if she can tear *that* in half! This is rather more difficult, if not impossible! Ask a second volunteer to break one twig in half. When he has done so, give him a large bundle of twigs that has been tightly tied together – ask him if he can break *that* in half.

Explain to the group that God wants us to meet regularly with other Christians to share in prayer, Bible study and fellowship. We need the support of other believers to give us the strength to continue growing in our faith. It's easy to tear up one piece of paper, but it's almost impossible to tear up a telephone directory. It's not difficult to break one twig, but it's hard to break a bundle of twigs. When Christians are part of a church, they are strengthened by the support of the other members of the congregation. Christians who try to go it alone often fall by the wayside; but those who meet regularly with other Christians have the support and encouragement they need to help them continue in the faith. There is strength in numbers.

> Let us be concerned for one another, to help one
> another to show love and to do good. Let us
> not give up the habit of meeting together, as
> some are doing. *(Hebrews 10:24–25)*

9 The Balloon that won't Pop!

If you stick a pin in a balloon, it will certainly burst! But if you put a piece of sticky tape over the balloon and then stick a pin into it through the tape, you will find that it doesn't burst but instead will maintain its shape for quite some time. The balloon is strengthened by the sticky tape and given the ability to withstand several pinpricks.

God can give us the strength we need to hold our own in times of trouble. When we face difficult situations, he is always ready to help us. He will give us the strength to cope with all the hard knocks and painful pinpricks life may send our way. Just as the sticky tape strengthened the balloon, so God gives strength to all who believe in him.

> God is our shelter and strength,
> always ready to help in times of trouble.
> *(Psalm 46:1)*

10 Hidden in the Heart

For this experiment you will need a paper heart-shape, the juice of a lemon, a paintbrush, an iron and ironing board.

In advance, cut a large sheet of paper into a heart-shape. Using the juice of a lemon, paint a selection of good and bad qualities on the heart, eg peace, patience, hate, anger, joy, love, kindness, anger, short temper, generosity, greed. Put the heart to one side and leave the lemon juice to dry. When the children arrive, show them the paper heart and explain that although it appears to be quite clean and white you are going to show them what this heart is really like. Take a very hot iron and press over the heart until the words appear. By a chemical process the lemon juice will go brown long before the paper does, so you will be able to read the writing.

When Samuel was sent to anoint the next king of Israel, he discovered that God doesn't judge people by their outward appearance but by what they are like on the inside. To Samuel's astonishment God didn't choose the oldest or the tallest or the most handsome of Jesse's sons to be the next king. Instead he chose David, the youngest, because he knew what David was like deep down inside and he was pleased with what he saw (1 Samuel 16:7).

God knows exactly what we're like. He can see both the good and bad things that are part of our personality: the love and the hate, the generosity and the greed, the honesty and the lies. There's nothing we can hide from him, because he knows us inside and out.

> Lord, you have examined me and you know me.
> You know everything I do;
> from far away you understand all my
> thoughts.
> You see me, whether I am working or resting;
> you know all my actions.
> Even before I speak,
> you already know what I will say.
> You are all round me on every side;
> you protect me with your power.
> Your knowledge of me is too deep;
> it is beyond my understanding.
> *(Psalm 139:1–6)*

8 Ten simple party games

Parties are a wonderful way to make new friendships and to cement old ones. It's great to have the chance to play a few silly games just for the fun of it and to meet with the children on a different footing.

If you only have a very small group of children, why not a have a 'Bring a Friend' party? A few extra children will make the games more exciting, and you may find that one or two of the visitors would like to join your weekly group.

When?

Many groups have an annual Christmas party; but if December is already far too hectic, what about one in the New Year? Alternatively, some children find the last couple of weeks of the summer holidays hard to fill, and a party is just what's needed to give everyone a boost. The advantage of a party in late August or early September is that it can be a way of re-launching your children's activities before the return to school in September.

You may like to consider 31 October as a possibility. Many children are invited to special Hallowe'en parties on this date. As Christians we don't want our children to get involved in such activities, but neither do we want to be spoilsports. Traditional Hallowe'en parties celebrate the forces of darkness, so an alternative would be to hold a 'Jesus is Light' or a rainbow party. Invite the children to wear bright clothes; have a few fireworks; play silly games by torchlight; eat hamburgers and hot dogs; and close with a short 'epilogue'.

Where?

If you have a small group, it may be a good idea to hold the party in a leader's home. You will find that it's easier to get to know the children better in a completely different setting. If you are a church group, there may be a member of the congregation with a suitable home who would be willing to host the party for you. Ask one or two children to come early to help lay out the food, and ask for volunteers to stay behind at the end to help clear up. If your party is being hosted by a member of the congregation, organise a small 'thank you' present and a card signed by the members of the group.

With a large group you may find it easier to hold your party in the church or school hall. Decorate the hall beforehand with lots of balloons, which could be used later in a game, and home-made streamers cut from crepe paper. For maximum effect, change white light bulbs for coloured ones.

Invitations

Invitation by word-of-mouth isn't enough: children love to have proper invitations, and it's even better if they arrive by post. Invitations also provide parents with the times they must deliver and pick up their offspring, plus any other important information. The examples below may give you ideas for possible designs. You could also use the 'Gobsmacked Message Cards' in section 4:6; or ask a friend with a computer to help you create your own. If you have decided to have a 'Bring a Friend' party, give each child an extra invitation to pass on to someone else.

Theme parties

It's often helpful to have a party with a theme, as this will help you decide on all the other aspects of the party. For example, you might choose to follow a colour, say yellow. Send yellow invitations; ask your guests to dress in yellow; decorate the room with yellow balloons and streamers; have yellow napkins, paper plates and cups; put yellow icing on the cakes; wrap the prizes in yellow gift-wrap; play games to the tune of 'We all live on a yellow submarine'!

At Christmas the children could come dressed as a nativity character, say a shepherd. Send sheep-shaped invitations; make sheep-shaped biscuits; wrap up the refreshments in a spotted hankie to represent a shepherd's picnic tea; play 'Find the Shepherd's Crook' or 'Find the Lost Sheep'. For entertainment, show the Scripture Union video *The Grumpy Shepherd*.

Older children enjoy a Christmas party in the heat of summer and a summer party in the lead-up to Christmas! For a summer party in December, invite the children to wear their favourite beachwear; borrow some travel posters from a local travel agent; have a knobbly-knee competition or a competition to make a sun-hat out of a sheet of newspaper and three paper-clips. Eat choc ices and play damp games like apple dunking and wet and watery obstacle races to the tune of 'We're all going on a summer holiday'.

Food

Don't be afraid to ask a friend or a member of the congregation to help with the shopping and preparation. And, if possible, invite a couple of extra adults just to serve and clear away the refreshments. Supermarkets today have a wide variety of special party food available, so if you're short of time, give someone a budget and ask them to pick out a suitable selection of pizza slices, sausage rolls and other appropriate party fare. You may find that the children would rather have sausage and chips than all sorts of fiddly nibbly things! In which case, put a pile of sausages in the oven at the beginning of the party and send someone out for chips! Choc ices make an excellent hassle-free dessert!

Organising games

If party games are not your forte, ask a friend or a member of the youth club to be chief games-master. The more extra leaders you have, the more smoothly your party will run. Have a good variety of different games – some energetic, some quiet and some creative: that is, something to appeal to all tastes. Avoid games like 'Musical Chairs' and 'Musical Statues' where children have to sit down when they're out. It's hard to maintain discipline when there are more children sitting out than left playing the game! Make sure you have a couple of games in reserve – one quiet and one noisy – in case you run out of ideas or want to change tempo quickly. With a large group it's essential to keep the children happily occupied the whole time. Plenty of games and precision timing is the key to success. You'll have no trouble with discipline if the children don't have time to get bored.

Games are sometimes difficult at the beginning of a party, when some children arrive early and others late. You don't want the early birds to get bored and you don't want the latecomers to miss the start of a game. It's a good idea to organise a special game that the children can join in as they arrive, so that no one is left waiting around for things to happen. With older children, a guessing game based on cards or pictures pinned up around the room works well. Simply give each child a pencil and paper as they arrive and send them off to look at the clues (see 'Find the Fault'). With younger children try a simple game such as pinning the tail on the donkey. To bring this game right up-to-date, you might want to try 'Fix the beak on Pingu', 'Stick the nose on Spot' or 'Pin the hat on Paddington'. At Christmas you could *Blu-tack* the red nose on Rudolph!

It's always worth having some background music playing as the children arrive: this will create the right, friendly, welcoming atmosphere. If appropriate, ask a child to lend you some up-to-date chart music.

Don't wait until all the children are bored to conclude a game. It's always a good idea to leave them wanting more. You can always offer to play a game again at the end, if there's still time.

If possible, timetable a lively game (to help the children let off steam) before you want them to sit down to eat. If you can go outside, that's even better. Organise a quiet game after tea, as accidents can happen when children are encouraged to run around on a full stomach!

Plan a special, well-organised game to play at the end when some parents might arrive early to collect their offspring. The parents will be impressed and you'll be more comfortable if everything is well under control and running super-smoothly at this stage!

1 Find the Fault

This is an ideal first game, as it provides the children with something to do as soon as they arrive. Photocopy and cut out the eight 'Find the Fault' cards on p 51. Pin these pictures around the room and, as the children arrive, give them pencil and paper; ask them to go round and jot down the mistake on each picture.

Answers

1 The back wheels are missing on one skateboard.
2 There are no black notes on the piano.
3 One bike has no chain on it.
4 The television isn't plugged in.
5 The teapot has no handle.
6 The date on the calendar doesn't exist.
7 The parasol has no support.
8 The car has no steering wheel.

✖ Cross Reference

Some of the activities suggested in section 1 make excellent introductory games for a party.

2 Wacky Races

Kipper

Divide the children into teams. Give each team a large paper fish and a folded newspaper. Each child wafts the paper fish to the end of the room by flapping the newspaper up and down behind it. The child then runs back to the team and gives the fish and newspaper to the next team member, who does the same. The game continues until the whole team has raced the fish to the end of the room. The first team to finish wins.

Orange Slalom

Each team member pushes an orange along the floor with his or her nose! To make the race a little more interesting, use skittles or large plastic bottles as markers, and insist that the orange must be pushed around a slalom course and back to the team. Award time penalties to anyone who hits a marker with his orange! The team with the fastest time wins.

Blow Football

This race is similar to 'Orange Slalom', but this time the team members use drinking straws to blow ping-pong balls around the markers.

Stepping Stones

Divide the children into teams, and give each team two sheets of card (A4 size works well). When the game starts, the first team member runs up to the end of the room, around a chair, and back again without touching the floor, using the cards as stepping stones. He then gives the cards to the next team member, who does the same. The first team to finish in the shortest time wins.

Cash in the Bottle

Divide the children into teams, and give each child a small coin, eg a two-pence piece. Place a milk bottle in front of each team, at the opposite end of the room. In turn, team members make their way to the milk bottles, gripping the coins between their knees. If anyone drops a coin on the way, she must return and try again. When the players reach the end of the room, they must drop the coins into their team's milk bottle without using their hands. The first team to finish in the shortest time wins.

3 Crazy Obstacle Races

Use tables, chairs, benches, hoops and blankets to set up two simple obstacle courses, side by side. If you have a large number of children and want to divide them into more than two teams, you will need to set up extra obstacle courses. In a typical race, children could crawl under a table, walk along a bench, wriggle under a blanket, weave in and out of a row of chairs and, finally, climb through a hoop to complete the course.

To make the obstacle race a little more interesting, you could combine it with one of the following ideas.

Balloon Challenge

Give each team a balloon and get the children to complete the obstacle course with a partner, holding the balloon between their two foreheads. If they drop the balloon, they must start again. If any team has an odd number in it, ask one child to run twice.

Balance the Books

This time the children complete the course one by one, balancing books on their heads. If you are able to play this game outside, substitute the book for a plastic tumbler of water!

Blindfold

The children complete the course with a partner, but one of the pair is blindfolded. The partner who can see must guide the other around the course.

Potato and Spoon

Exactly as the title suggests! Get each child to complete the obstacle course balancing a potato on a tablespoon.

4 Animal Talk

This is a particularly silly, noisy game, but it's great fun! In advance, hide two or three packets of wrapped sweets all around the room(s) you are meeting in. Make sure some are well hidden. Divide the children into groups of four or five, and give each group an animal name and a noise to make, eg dogs – 'Woof woof'; ducks – 'Quack quack'; sheep – 'Baa baa'; cats – 'Miaow miaow'; cows – 'Moo moo'. Give one child in each group a paper bag in which to collect the sweets: he or she is the only one in the group allowed to pick them up. All the others must look for the sweets and then attract their collector's attention by making the appropriate animal noise. The sweets can be divided between each group at the end of the game.

5 Test the Senses

You can either play all three parts of this game or just stick to one section. If you have three leaders available, ask each one to prepare a tray of things to identify.

Guess the Smell

The first leader must prepare ten small pots for the children to guess the contents by their smell. As each child arrives at the leader's table he puts on a blindfold. The leader then holds up a pot for the child to identify the smell. Suitable smells include lemon, onion, coffee, vanilla, TCP, cinnamon, garlic, toothpaste, almond essence, vinegar, nutmeg, cheese, blackcurrant juice, mixed herbs. The child whispers his answers to the leader who keeps track of how many are right, jotting down the score on a score-card which the child then takes with him to the next stage of the game.

Guess the Taste

The second leader prepares a similar set of ten pots, but this time the children have to guess the contents by the taste. Suitable tasters include, bread, cold mashed potato, cooked parsnip, raw carrot, banana, chocolate, lettuce, cucumber, mayonnaise, tomato ketchup, yoghurt, crisps (insist on knowing the flavours of the last two). It's just as well to check that none of the children suffer from any food allergies before you play this part of the game.

Guess the Feel

The last leader prepares a selection of about ten things for the children to guess by their feel. All the objects are placed on a table and covered with a huge tablecloth. The children must feel each object through the material and guess its identity. Suitable objects include a tin opener, a piece of Lego, a tube of toothpaste, a pocket calculator, a computer disk, a roll of Sellotape, a battery, a paper-clip, a clothes-peg, a whisk, a bunch of keys, an orange, a cassette case, a comb, a hole-puncher.

The child with the highest combined score from all three stages is the winner, although if you're feeling generous you could award a prize to the child with the best score in each. If you want to make it more difficult for older children, let them go to each table and smell, taste or feel all the items but, after each stage, send them away to write down as many items as they can remember.

The game works well with groups of ten or twelve. It is probably not a good idea to play with a huge number of children, since relatively few youngsters can be actively engaged at any one time.

6 Potato People

This a creative game that often makes a pleasant change of tempo in the middle of a hectic party.

Give the children a large potato each, and have available a selection of sticky shapes, cotton wool, pipe-cleaners, scraps of material and coloured paper, plus a number of spent matchsticks which can be used to attach materials to the potato. Invite the children to use all the materials to create their own potato person. Provide sticky labels so that they can name their creations. Display the finished potato people, and award prizes for creativity, humour, fashion, ingenuity, and so on. Let the children take their potato creations home with them. They can always be turned into baked potatoes at a later date!

✖ CROSS REFERENCE

Other craft projects might include 'Make a party hat', section 1:3; or 'Balloon characters', section 2:2.

7 Drawing Game

For this game, divide the children into groups of five or six. Give each group a few sheets of paper and a pencil. The groups should be spaced around the room, preferably out of earshot of each other. If this isn't possible, encourage the children to whisper. The leader stands in the centre with a list of about twenty things to draw. Each group sends one member to hear the first item. She then comes back and draws it for the rest of the group to guess. She isn't allowed to write any words or letters on the page, neither can she speak: she can only nod or shake her head. When a team member makes a correct guess, that team member goes to the leader, whispers the answer and receives a second item to draw for the team. The game continues in this way until one group finishes the whole list.

The list should include a selection of quite precise things to draw, eg an oak tree, a tin-opener, a post office, jelly and ice cream, Big Ben, a tin of baked beans, a skateboard, a cheese-and-tomato pizza, a telephone directory, a vase of daffodils, a double-decker bus, a birthday cake, a scarecrow, the weather man on TV, a four-poster bed, an alarm clock, a fire engine, a bride and groom, an advent calendar, a combine harvester.

8 Three Games for a Circle of Chairs

SQUEAK, PIGGY, SQUEAK!

This is an old favourite that is often forgotten. It works best when all the children know each other quite well, otherwise the guessing involved is completely impossible! The children sit in a circle and one child stands in the centre. He is blindfolded, given a cushion and then turned round three times before setting off to find someone in the circle. When he finds someone, he puts the cushion on that child's lap, sits on it and says 'Squeak, piggy, squeak!' The child who is being squashed squeaks, and the blindfolded child has to guess who it is. If he guesses correctly, he swaps places and the other child goes into the middle.

ALL CHANGE!

This is a fairly simple game which can help younger children let off steam in an organised fashion! The children sit on chairs arranged in a huge circle, but there should be one less chair than the number of children. The remaining child stands in the centre. The leader calls out the names of two children who have to change places with each other. The child in the middle must run to grab one of the vacated seats so that one of the other two is left standing in the middle. Every so often the leader shouts out, 'All change!' at which point everyone tries to change places with everyone else.

MOVE ALONG NOW, PLEASE!

Make a tight circle of chairs, with one chair for each child. Ask a volunteer to stand in the centre. Explain to the children that if the chair on their left becomes vacant they must move to it. This means that all the children are constantly moving on by one seat. The child in the centre must try to sit on a seat as soon as it becomes vacant. This isn't as easy as it sounds! If he succeeds, the child who is now without a seat goes into the middle. Every so often the leader can shout, 'Change direction!' at which point the children move to the seat on their right.

☞ TIP

It's important that the chairs are arranged in a tight circle, or you will find that children will fall through the gaps.

9 Two Laughing Games

GOOD NIGHT, TEDDY

This game is quite ridiculous, but great fun! Have ready a child's dressing-gown, some kind of nightcap and a big teddy bear. Each child has to put on the dressing-gown and nightcap, then hug the teddy and say as seriously as he or she can, 'Dear Teddy, darling Teddy, good night! Sleep tight!' The only rule is that she isn't allowed to laugh while she says this! You will find that it's almost impossible to play the game without laughing, but it's great fun to watch everyone struggle to keep a straight face. You might like to award a small prize to the player who is the most convincing!

Team Challenge

Divide the children into two teams. The first team stands in a line while the second team stands no less than a metre away and pulls faces, tells jokes and tries all the tricks they can think of to make the other team laugh. They have up to two minutes to get all the other team out. Any member of the first team who smiles, laughs or giggles must sit down. Use a stopwatch to time how long the first team hold out, then swap the teams round. The winning team is the one which lasts the longest.

10 Six Quieter Games

It's always a good idea to have one or two quiet games ready that you can use if the children get just a bit too noisy and overexcited. It spoils the party atmosphere if you have to keep shouting, 'Calm down!' or 'Be quiet!', and it leaves you feeling very frazzled. It's far more effective to include a couple of quick, quiet games in the programme and to have one or two others in reserve.

Sleeping Lions

Play some lively music and let the children leap around for a minute or two. When the music stops, they all lie down on the floor and close their eyes. Explain that they are all sleeping lions. There's a hunter on the prowl who is looking for lions, but he's rather short-sighted and will only notice lions that move. The aim of the game is for the children to lie completely still for as long as possible. Anyone who moves is out and can come and join you as you observe the remaining lions. No touching is allowed, but those who are out can try and make the others move by making daft comments, eg 'There's a spider crawling up your left leg!'

Teapotting

This is a simple word game that is easy to pick up and great fun to play. All the children sit in a circle. Explain that you are going to think of a verb (You might to need to refer to it as 'a doing word' or a word that can sometimes end with 'ing'). Invite the children to guess the word by asking simple questions that can be answered with 'Yes' or 'No'. However, in their questions they must substitute the word 'teapot' for the unknown verb, eg 'Do people *teapot* every day?' 'Can you go *teapotting* in the rain?' 'Do you *teapot* indoors?' 'Do some people *teapot* in the bath?' 'Do you need any special clothing for *teapotting*?'

Guess a Minute

This game is so simple that it is a sheer delight! Ask the children to lie down, relax and close their eyes. Explain that you are going to time them for one minute and you want them to guess how long a minute lasts. All they have to do is raise a finger and leave it up when they think that a minute has passed. The game continues until everyone has registered their guess. You can award a sweet to the child whose guess was closest to an actual minute. You should find that the children are as quiet as mice and some won't register their guess until almost two minutes have passed. With older children, you may want to ask them to guess 90 seconds or even two minutes. Don't worry if it all seems rather pointless; this game has only one objective – to calm the children down!

The Bear and the Honeypot

This game is particularly popular with younger children. Seat the group in a circle and invite one child to be the bear and wear a blindfold. He must sit in the centre with a jar of honey beside him. Explain that the bear finds it difficult to sleep at night because he is worried that someone will steal his honey. Choose another child sitting in the circle to have a go at stealing the honey. She must tiptoe around the circle and into the centre to grab the jar of honey before the bear wakes up. If the bear hears her coming and points directly at her, she is out and someone else has a go. If, however, she is successful and steals the honey before the bear 'wakes up', she can swap places with the bear who then goes to sit in the circle with the others.

Drawing on Heads

Give the children a book, a pencil and a piece of paper each, and ask them to place the paper on their heads, using the book to rest on. Tell them that you want them to draw a picture on the paper they have on their heads. Make the picture quite detailed, and keep going back to add something new to earlier parts of the picture which the children will find quite difficult. You will find that they draw many things on top of each other, and the result is amusing chaos. The instructions could go something like this:

- Draw a picture of a house.
- The house has a front door and four windows, two upstairs and two downstairs.
- There's a chimney on the right hand side of the roof.
- Draw an apple tree in the garden to the left of the house.
- There is smoke coming out of the chimney.
- Draw a car outside the house.
- There's a man standing beside the car.
- He is looking at a child who is watching from an upstairs window, the window on the right.
- The man is holding an umbrella because it's raining…

When all the pictures are finished, pass them round and let everyone have a good laugh! This isn't a competitive game, although you could give sweets to the child who has drawn the most recognisable picture. Even better, give everyone a sweet just for taking part.

Ring on a String

Thread a curtain ring onto a long piece of string, and tie the two ends of the string together to make a circle. You will need to make the circle of string big enough for all the children to hold with both hands. The aim of the game is to secretly pass the ring around the circle. The children should clench their hands together and slide them from side to side along the string, so that they are ready to receive the ring when it comes round. One child has to stand in the centre, he shuts his eyes and counts to twenty before guessing who has the ring hidden in their hands. The ring can keep moving the whole time. Once he has guessed correctly, the child in the middle swaps places with the child hiding the ring. The aim of the game is to find the ring using the fewest number of guesses.

FIND THE FAULT
1
2
3
4
5
6
30 FEB
7
8

9 Ten ideas for creative prayer

All too often adults pray on behalf of children and it becomes a question of 'Hands together and eyes closed, and don't forget to join in when I say "Amen" at the end!' Many children must grow up assuming that prayer is something done by someone else, and unaware of the fact that God loves his children to speak to him individually as well as in groups. How can we expect children to learn to pray if we don't let them join in from the start? It's all too easy to switch off when someone else is praying (even adults do it). Children are quite capable of praying for themselves, and their prayers often show an understanding that would surprise many adults. However, if leaders always pray at great length and pepper their prayers with long and learned words, those listening may well be left feeling 'I could never do that!'

It is important, therefore, that we find ways of encouraging children to pray both on their own and in small groups. We don't need to limit ourselves to spoken prayers: we can also write and draw our special prayers for God. Sometimes drawing something for which we want to thank God can make us stop, think and take a little more time over our prayer. Moreover, younger children often find it easier to express themselves in a picture than in written words. So let's be creative in our prayer and worship.

1 A Bouquet of Flowers

...offer him glorious praise. *(Psalm 66:2)*

Have you ever given someone a bunch of flowers on a special occasion? Well, why not make some special prayer-flowers for God? Use the template on p 60 to cut flower shapes from coloured paper. Then invite the children to write or draw something on their shapes for which they would like to thank God. Stick the finished prayer-flowers to a sheet of backing paper. Add a few drinking straws or lengths of green paper to represent stalks, and cut a few leaves out of green paper. Finally, say a short prayer offering the whole bouquet to God.

2 Trefoil (Thank you, Sorry, Please)

'Lord, teach us to pray...' *(Luke 11:1)*

Children often comment that they just don't know what to pray about. Sometimes it's helpful to explain that many prayers can be based on the words 'Thank you', 'Sorry' and 'Please' which have all been incorporated into the following prayer-trefoil.

Draw a large outline of a simple trefoil, or shamrock, so that the three leaves are quite distinct. Label one of the leaves 'THANK YOU', one of them 'SORRY' and the other 'PLEASE'. Have available plenty of sticky labels so that the children can write short one-line prayers, eg 'Thank you for keeping us safe as we travelled on holiday', 'Please, God, help my gran to get well soon', or 'Sorry, Lord, that I was bad-tempered with everyone yesterday'. Younger children who cannot write confidently should be encouraged to draw their prayers. Invite the group to stick their prayers to the appropriate leaf on the trefoil. Conclude with a short prayer offering the whole prayer-picture to God.

☞ TIP

Address labels are just the right size for a one-line prayer, but if you want to re-use the trefoil over and over again, let the children write their prayers on post-it notes.

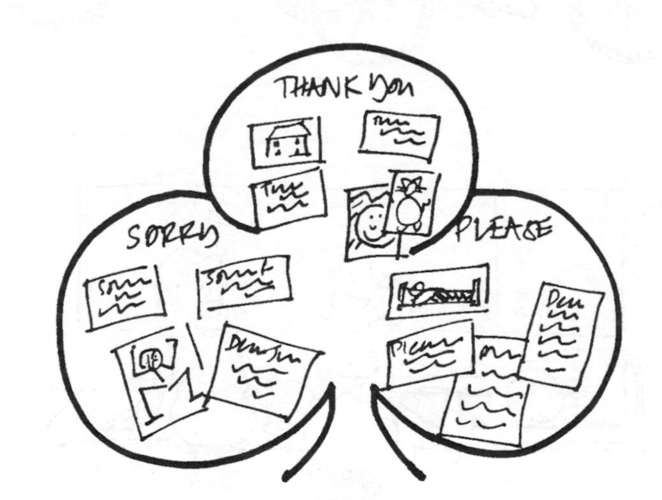

3 In the Bin

'I will forgive their sins
and will no longer remember their wrongs.'
(Hebrews 8:12)

Discuss with your group some of the things that we often do that must make God feel very sad. Write your ideas on a large sheet of paper. Expect suggestions like fighting with brothers/sisters, telling lies, being grumpy, not helping at home, stealing, swearing, being naughty. Use a marker pen to write the suggestions on a large sheet of paper. Once the sheet is full, pray a short prayer in which you group the children's suggestions together into a simple response-prayer. Explain that you would like them to say, 'Sorry, Lord' every time they hear the cue 'We really want to say...'. For example:

For fighting and telling lies,
We really want to say…
Sorry, Lord.
For swearing and stealing,
We really want to say…
Sorry, Lord.
For being grumpy and bad-tempered,
We really want to say…
Sorry, Lord.
For the times when we're naughty and refuse to help,
We really want to say…
Sorry, Lord.
For all the things we do that make you feel sad,
We really want to say…
Sorry, Lord.
Amen.

When the prayer is finished, slowly and deliberately tear the sheet of paper into small pieces and drop them into a waste bin. As you do this, explain that when we say sorry to God, he is always ready not only to forgive us but also to forget about all the things we have done wrong. It's as if God tears up all our wrongdoing and throws it in the bin, then gives us the opportunity to make a fresh start.

4 Forgiven and Washed Clean

Be merciful to me, O God,
because of your constant love.
Because of your great mercy
wipe away my sins!
Wash away all my evil
and make me clean from my sin!
(Psalm 51:1–2)

As in 'In the Bin', ask your group to help you write a list of some of the things that we do that must make God feel sad. Use a water-soluble pen to write your suggestions on an OHP acetate. Once the list is complete, weave all the suggestions into a simple response-prayer similar to the example given below. Invite the children to join in with the response 'Please forgive us and wash us clean' every time they hear the cue 'Father God…'

We are sorry, Lord, for all the things we do that make you feel sad.
Father God…
Please forgive us and wash us clean.
We are sorry for the times when we lie and cheat.
Father God…
Please forgive us and wash us clean.
We are sorry for the times when we are grumpy, selfish or unkind.
Father God…
Please forgive us and wash us clean.
We are sorry for the times when we are naughty and disobedient.
Father God…
Please forgive us and wash us clean.
We are sorry for the times when we fight or argue with our brothers, sisters and friends.
Father God…
Please forgive us and wash us clean.
We do so many things that we know are wrong.
Father God…
Please forgive us and wash us clean.
Amen.

When the response-prayer is finished, gently sprinkle two or three drops of water onto the words on the acetate, and watch the ink dissolve in the water. Then wipe the whole acetate clean with a damp cloth. (Take great care not to flood the OHP; it is, after all, an electrical appliance!) Finally, make the point that when God forgives our sins, he also forgets them and washes them away, making us clean on the inside and giving us the opportunity to make a fresh start.

5 Shopping Trolley (Harvest)

He gives food to every living creature;
his love is eternal. *(Psalm 136:25)*

The following prayer-collage is particularly suitable for use at harvest time when it can be displayed in church as a focus for prayer.

Collect a number of food magazines, supermarket leaflets and food advertisements. Invite the children to cut out pictures of their favourite foods and paste them to a sheet of paper within the outline of a shopping trolley. Point out that though we buy our food in shops and supermarkets everything we eat has first been provided by God. Look at the list of ingredients on one or two packets and tins, and work out how various products first started life. When the food-collage is finished, add the caption 'Thank you, Lord, for all the good things you give us to eat'. Finally, take a moment to pray and offer the finished collage to God.

6 Prayer People

…pray always for all God's people.
(Ephesians 6:18)

Cut out a number of gingerbread-men shapes (a template is provided on p 61), enough for all the children in your group. Explain that God likes us to pray for the particular needs of our friends, neighbours and families. Invite the children to use the shapes to write short prayers for particular people they know for whom they would like to pray. Stick all the finished prayers to the wall with *Blu-tack*. You could arrange the shapes to form a long line or a pyramid. In subsequent weeks, take another look at the prayers. Thank God for answered prayers and continue to pray for those situations that still cause concern. Have ready some blank shapes so that children can add new prayers to the collection.

7 Bunting

This is the day of the Lord's victory;
let us be happy, let us celebrate!
(Psalm 118:24)

Give each member of your group a coloured paper triangle and invite them to write a one-line 'thank you' prayer. Fasten all the triangles to a length of ribbon to make a festive string of bunting that you can hang across your meeting room. If your group is small you may want to give them two or three triangles each, or you could add to the bunting week by week. Prayer bunting is particularly effective on special occasions like Christmas, Easter, church anniversaries or holiday club services, when an extra long string can be made during an all-age service.

8 Heartfelt Praise

I thank you, Lord, with all my heart...
(Psalm 138:1)

Cut out a heart-shaped piece of paper for each member of your group (a template is provided on p 60). Punch a hole in the centre at the top of the heart and attach a piece of cotton or embroidery thread. Explain that God loves us with all of his heart and he is overjoyed when his people return this love. God has given so many good things to us and done so many wonderful things for us that he deserves our love and praise. Invite each child to write a short one-line prayer on his or her heart-shape. Then string up all the hearts from a curtain pole or a length of string tied across a corner of your meeting room. As the children bring up their hearts to add to the display, sing a song joyfully but prayerfully, eg 'We are here to praise You' by Graham Kendrick (Kingsway's Thankyou Music, 1985), *Songs of Fellowship* no 567.

9 Thank You, Lord

He lets me rest in fields of green grass
and leads me to quiet pools of fresh water.
(Psalm 23:2)

All too often adults say prayers on behalf of children without really considering the kinds of things they might like to pray for. The following prayer is about holidays, but the idea can be used for many other topics, eg family and friends, favourite food, things that make us feel happy.

Invite the group to tell you some of the things they have enjoyed during the holidays. Make a list of their suggestions on a sheet of paper or OHP acetate. Then weave their ideas into a prayer where they join in with the response 'Thank you, Lord' every time they hear the cue 'We really want to say...' In this way the children are participating twice, by suggesting prayer topics and by joining in with a response.

For lazy days and holidays
We really want to say...
Thank you Lord.
For swimming and cycling and day trips out
We really want to say...
Thank you Lord.
For camping and caravanning
We really want to say...
Thank you, Lord.
For the fun of visiting new places
We really want to say...
Thank you, Lord.
For the time to play with friends
We really want to say...
Thank you, Lord.
Amen.

10 Prayer Wall

First of all, then, I urge that petitions, prayers,
requests, and thanksgivings be offered to God
for all people. *(1 Timothy 2:1)*

On a sheet of A4 or A3 size paper, draw a section of a wall, about 14 bricks. If there is a suitably rough wall nearby, place the sheet against it and lightly rub with a pencil: this will help to create the right 'brick' texture. But leave a blank area in the middle of each brick for the children to write in their prayers.

Photocopy enough copies to give one to each group of six to eight children. Give each group a selection of felt-tipped pens and invite them to write their prayer requests to God on the bricks. They could write about personal needs, eg 'Dear Lord, please keep us safe as we travel on holiday', or about the needs of their friends and relatives, eg 'Father God, please help my grandad to feel better soon'. As far as possible have a leader work with each group so that prayer requests can be discussed before they are written on the wall. Once the wall is complete, allow a little time for children to pray about the items written on it.

If you have a large number of groups, all the sections of wall can be joined together to make one long wall. Alternatively, with a small group you might like to add further sections to the wall in subsequent weeks.

From time to time, take a few moments to review the prayer wall. Thank God for answered prayers and pray again for items that are still topical. You may find it helpful to explain to the children that God answers some prayers with an immediate 'Yes', other prayers he answers 'No', and some prayers he answers, 'Wait', because this isn't the right time. It's rather like a set of traffic lights where green represents 'Go' or 'Yes ', red represents 'Stop' or 'No' and amber 'Wait'. Point out that just as all the bricks work together to make the whole wall strong, so individual prayers make a church strong.

✖ Cross Reference
It's worth checking out 'Windmills', section 4:1.

10 Ten half-hour programmes

The following programmes combine a selection of ideas from the previous nine sections in the book. You probably won't want to use these programmes word for word, so feel free to adapt the activities to suit your group and situation. Try to put together a balanced programme, just as you would select a balanced meal in a restaurant. Don't spend too long on any one activity, but offer three or four different things within your half-hour session. Children get bored very easily, so it's often a good idea to offer several short activities rather than one long one. Individual children enjoy different things and have completely different needs. As far as possible, try to select a programme that includes some quiet activities and some noisy ones, some discussion and some listening, something creative and something active.

Don't be afraid to play a game just for the sake of it – it helps children to use up some of their excess energy, so that they can then sit down and listen to a story more attentively.

Aims and introductions

Try to decide on an aim for each session. After all, if you aim at nothing that's certainly what you will achieve! Read through the Bible story you intend to use, and ask God what he wants to teach you and what he would like the children to learn. Take another look at the paragraph 'Why?' in the introduction to section 2 on 'Telling a Bible story'.

Next, think how you are going to introduce the topic. Perhaps you need an introductory activity to help build a bridge between the world of the child and the world of the Bible. Sometimes it can be quite a culture shock for a child to sit down and listen to a Bible story. The story of Jesus washing the disciples feet makes no sense at all to a child who doesn't understand that in Bible times people walked around barefoot or in open sandals. So it was great to have your feet washed and be able sit down to a meal in comfort. In this case a suitable introductory activity might be to play a game barefoot and then to stop and wash all the dirty feet before listening to how Jesus did the very same thing. This might sound like a huge hassle, but you can be sure that this is one story they won't forget and they will be sure to tell the folks at home how they washed their feet in today's session!

Bible story

There are many different ways of putting over a Bible story. You could use mime, drama or even a video. Alternatively, you could tell the story with pictures or sound effects or a particular response. Ten different approaches have been suggested in section 2, and there are plenty more besides. Try not to use the same approach every week, but surprise the children with something fresh and exciting.

Application

Once you have told the Bible story, it's a good idea to include an activity that draws out how that particular story applies to the lives of the children: this will probably be reflected in your choice of aim. Thus, after telling the story of the storm on the lake and hearing how the disciples turned to Jesus when they were afraid, we might want to go on to discuss some of the times when we often feel afraid; times when, in future, we can ask Jesus to be especially close to us.

Responding to God

Finally, it's important to give the children the opportunity to respond to all God has been teaching them. The response might be in prayer, praise, music, or any kind of creative, musical or artistic worship. Encourage the children to respond to God in whatever way they feel best able to express their feelings. Try to avoid simply saying a prayer on behalf of the children and asking them to join in with the word 'Amen' at the end. Take another look at section 9.

Memory verses

A suitable memory verse to go with each of the suggested Bible stories can be found at the beginning of section 5.

The SALT programme

SALT stands for 'Sharing And Learning Together'. Scripture Union's SALT programme offers a weekly selection of activities for groups that meet on Sundays or mid-week. The material is aimed at children aged 3 to 13+ in four different, co-ordinated, age bands: 3 to 4+, 5 to 7+, 8 to 10+, and 11 to 13+, with a special activity magazine for each age group. Additional material for adults and all-age worship suggestions are offered in an All-Age magazine.

Each week you are offered a 'pick 'n' mix' menu. You simply select the stories, games, activities and worship ideas that would best suit your group. All the activities combine together to create a well-balanced programme with four different sections: 'Way In', 'Bible', 'Life' and 'Response'. The SALT syllabus covers all the major themes of the Bible and explores some of the key issues facing Christians today. If you would like more information and a free sample, write to Scripture Union's Sales & Marketing Dept (address on p 64).

1 Christmas

Aim

- To hear how the shepherds heard about the birth of Jesus and then shared the good news with others.
- To think how we can share the real meaning of Christmas with our friends.

Opening Activity

Ask the children to help you make a list of all the words that come to mind when you say the word Christmas, eg turkey, holly, mince pies, cards, presents, Santa, Christmas carols, decorations, stable, angels, tinsel, glitter, parties.

Take a look at your list and put a circle round the words that have everything to do with our modern celebration of Christmas and nothing to do with Jesus' birthday. Point out that Christmas has become so commercialised that it's easy to forget that it's really Jesus' birthday we're celebrating. Explain that in this session you are going to go right back to the time when Jesus was first born, to when a group of shepherds heard about him for the very first time. In those days no one had ever heard of Christmas!

Bible Story

Luke 2:8–20: use 'Picture Story', section 2:1.

Application

When the shepherds left the stable after visiting the newborn baby Jesus, they were full of their exciting news. No doubt they hurried home to share the news with their families. Ask the children to imagine they have a friend from another country, who doesn't celebrate Christmas and doesn't know anything about Jesus. How would they share the news with this friend. Divide the children into small groups, and give them a few minutes to improvise a short sketch to show how they would explain the meaning of Christmas to someone who doesn't know what it's all about.

Response

Make some festive Christmas bunting, section 9:7. Encourage the children to write short prayers that are relevant to Christmas, eg 'Thank you for the gift of your Son', 'Thank you for Jesus' birthday', 'Thank you, Lord, for all the fun we have at Christmas'.

Extra Activities

If you have time, use 'Blockbusters', section 3:7; or make one of the Christmas decorations, section 4:9.

2 The Lost Sheep

Aim

- To discover that God loves every individual just as much and more than the shepherd loved his lost lamb.

Opening Activity

This activity is probably best suited to younger children. Pretend that you have lost something of great sentimental value, eg a wedding or an engagement ring, a locket, a photograph. Hide the lost object somewhere in your meeting room – make sure it's well hidden. Pretend to be very upset and ask the children to help you look for it. When the lost object has been found, explain that you are really happy to be reunited with it because it's very precious and quite irreplaceable. Thank your group for looking so thoroughly, and explain that in this week's story they're going to hear about someone who searched even more carefully for something precious that he had lost.

Bible Story

Luke 15:1–7, Matthew 18:12–14: use the 'A story with responses', section 2:4.

Application

Make sure the children understand that God loves us just as much as the shepherd loved his sheep. Sometimes we are just as foolish as that sheep – we go our own way and get lost. Ask the group to suggest some of the silly things we do that distance us from God. Fortunately, God cares about us very much indeed and is always ready to come looking for us, to reach out to us just like the shepherd in the story.

Help the children make sheep bookmarks with an appropriate verse or caption, section 5:10.

Response

On a photocopier, enlarge and make enough copies of the sheep template (p 60) for each child. Invite the children to write or draw a short 'thank you' prayer on their sheep, thanking God that he loves us like the shepherd in the story. Mount all the sheep on a sheet of backing paper, so that you have a flock of prayers!

3 The Good Samaritan

Aim

- To understand that God wants us to treat everyone with love, not just the people we like.

Opening Activity

Bring in a selection of magazines and ask the children to cut out lots of different faces – young and old, male and female, rich and poor, faces of all types and all nationalities. Paste the faces to a piece of backing paper to make a collage, leaving a space at the top to write the question 'Who is my neighbour?' Explain that today's story is one that Jesus once told to answer this very same question. Leave a space at the bottom of the collage to write the answer 'Everyone!' once you have told the story.

Bible Story

Luke 10:30–37: use the 'Acetate Story', section 2:7.

Application

Ask the children to think back over the story. Point out that it was the person the traveller may have least expected to help who actually stopped and treated him kindly (Jews and Samaritans weren't very friendly towards each other in those days). Ask the children to think how they might rewrite the story in a modern setting. The Riding Lights theatre group reset the story on a train between London and York. The traveller was mugged by a football fan and helped on his way by a good punk rocker! Divide the children into small groups to devise a sketch based on the story of the good Samaritan. Point out that Jesus wants us to show love to everyone and that includes people we don't much like.

Response

Sing the following:

- 'A new commandment that I give to you', Junior Praise no 303.
- 'When I needed a neighbour', Junior Praise no 275.

Conclude with a short prayer asking God to help the group members to show love towards everyone, not just to friends and family, but also to people that we don't like very much, or to people who are in some way different.

Extra Activity

Use 'Crossword Quiz', section 3:5.

4 The Two House Builders

Aim

- Jesus invites us to build our lives on him, and we must decide how to respond.

Opening Activity

Just for fun, bring in a selection of Lego or Duplo bricks or similar, and divide the children into small groups to build a house. After a few minutes, stop and take a look at the houses. Ask the children how much time they spent planning them? How strong do they think their house is? Can they think of any improvements? Children who have had a Lego base tray (foundation!) on which to build their houses will have been able to build something a little more stable.

Explain that this week's story is about two house builders, one who planned his house carefully and the other who started building without any plan at all.

Bible Story

Matthew 7:24–27, Luke 6:47–49: tell the story using the 'Balloon Characters', section 2:2.

Application

Help the children to make rectangular boxes, section 4:3. Take the opportunity to talk to them about the story while they are working. On one side write the caption 'Build your life on Jesus'. Don't glue down the lid of the box – the children will then be able to use it to keep bits and pieces in. Point out that the box is brick-shaped and will remind them about the story of the two house builders.

Explain that it's not enough to say you are going to build your life on Jesus; you also have to do something about it. Bring in some sample copies of children's Bible reading notes and explain that God wants us to read the Bible regularly and build our lives on his teaching.

Write to Scripture Union's Marketing Department (address on p 64) for details of *Let's Go!* (activity notes for 7–9s) and *Check it Out!* (Filofax-style notes for 9–11s).

Response

Since this story is about building, it may be appropriate to use a prayer wall to help the children respond to God, section 9:10. Allocate a blank brick to each child, and invite them to write short prayers asking God to help them build their lives on the foundation of his love and teaching, eg 'Lord, please help me to be like the wise man', or 'Father God, please help me to build my life on you'.

5 Zacchaeus meets Jesus

Aim

To discover how meeting Jesus can change your life.

Opening Activity

Use 'Washed Clean', section 7:4, to explain how Zacchaeus behaved before he met Jesus. Write the words 'lonely', 'greedy', 'unfair' and 'cheat' on the handkerchief, then immerse it in a bowl of hot soapy water to soak. Explain that in this session you are going to tell them how meeting Jesus changed a man called Zacchaeus completely, and all his greed, cheating and loneliness disappeared. Go back to the handkerchief after you have told the story, so that you can discover that all the bad qualities have been washed away.

Bible Story

Luke 19:2–9: use the sketch in 'Time to Act', section 2:6.

Application

Divide a sheet of paper in half and write the word 'BEFORE' on one side and the word 'AFTER' on the other. Ask the children to help you describe Zacchaeus before he met Jesus, eg he was lonely, sad and had no friends, he was a cheat, greedy and loved money more than people. Then ask the children to help you describe Zacchaeus *after* he had met Jesus: eg he was happy, overjoyed and had lots of friends; he was honest and generous. Point out that meeting Jesus made a big change to Zacchaeus' life. If we invite Jesus into our lives, we can be sure that it will be a life-changing experience too.

Response

Jesus forgave Zacchaeus for all the things he had done wrong, and gave him the opportunity to make a fresh start. In many ways we are just like Zacchaeus because we have all done wrong things. Use 'In the Bin', section 9:3.

6 The Storm on the Lake

Aim

- To hear how the disciples turned to Jesus when they were afraid, and to realise that we can do the same.

Opening Activity

On individual slips of paper, write down some of the things that make people feel afraid, eg the dark, fierce dogs, thunderstorms, heights, spiders, wasps. Ask for volunteers to come to the front and mime these things for the rest of the group to guess. At the end, explain that these are all things which make people feel frightened. This week we are going to hear how the disciples felt very scared when a fierce storm rocked the boat they were in.

Bible Story

Mark 4:35–41: use 'A Story with Sound Effects', section 2:3.

Application

Help the children to make a memory-verse spinner that will remind them of the message of this week's story, section 5:9. Write the words 'The Lord is with me, I will not be afraid' (Psalm 118:6) on one side of the card. Talk to the children about the story while they are cutting and colouring.

Response

Photocopy a gingerbread-man shape (p 61) for each child in your group. Invite the children to write or draw a short prayer on their shapes, asking God to be especially close to them at particular times when they feel afraid. Many children don't like to admit that there are things which make them feel frightened. Tell them you don't want to read these prayers – they are something quite secret, just between them and God; so they can write exactly what they like. If some children don't know what to write, you could suggest a simple prayer such as 'Lord Jesus, please be close to me when I'm afraid'. Collect the prayers in a box and offer them to God. Reassure the children that you don't intend to read them later.

Extra Activity

Write a number of quiz questions and organise a quick quiz based on the suggestions in 'Climb the Tree', section 3:4. Give each team a boat-shaped marker and draw a long wavy line to represent water. Divide the line into numbered sections and move the boats one step along the line for each correct answer.

7 Blind Bartimaeus

Aim

- To hear how Jesus noticed and healed a blind man, and to thank God for the gift of sight.

Opening Activity

Divide the children into pairs. Give one child in each pair a blindfold to put on. The child wearing the blindfold is guided around the room by his partner who can take him to speak to others whom the blindfolded child must identify by touch and hearing. After a few moments change over and let the partner wear the blindfold. The aim is for them to discover, in part, how it must feel to be blind. Explain that this week's story is about someone called Bartimaeus who was blind from birth.

Bible Story

Mark 10:46–52: use 'Draw a Story', section 2:10.

Application

Use the 'True/False Quiz', section 3:1. After the relevant questions, draw out in particular the following points:

Question 5:
Despite the huge crowd, Jesus noticed Bartimaeus and heard him calling. Jesus always notices what we are doing and will always hear us when we call to him.

Questions 8 & 9:
Bartimaeus had great faith in Jesus, and his faith and his persistence were rewarded. Jesus doesn't always heal people today, but he cares about people with disabilities and can give them the strength to cope. We know that in heaven everyone will have a new body and no one will suffer from any kind of disability.

Response

Ask the children to name some of the things they enjoy looking at: a beautiful view, rolling seas, green trees, golden daffodils, a favourite television programme, a smiling face. Make a list of their suggestions and weave them together to make a response prayer in the style of 'Thank You, Lord', section 9:9.

8 Mary and Martha Entertain a Special Visitor

Aim

- To discover the importance of spending time with Jesus and listening to him.

Opening Activity

Ask your group to imagine that someone very special is coming to supper with them. It could be their favourite pop star, or an actor, or a member of the royal family. Let them choose! Ask them to think what preparations they would make, how much cleaning they would do and what kind of meal they would prepare.

When the special guest arrives, how will they entertain him or her? Explain that in this story we are going to hear how a woman called Martha spent a great deal of time getting ready for a visit from Jesus. Unfortunately, when Jesus arrived, she was still frantically busy and hardly spent a moment with her special guest.

Bible Story

Luke 10:38–42: use 'Stand up, Turn round, Sit down', section 2:5.

Application

Help the children make a special helicopter that will remind them of the message of this week's story, section 4:2. Write the caption 'Don't whizz around all day! Remember to stop, listen and pray!' on one side of the helicopter.

Response

Read out James 4:8 – 'Come near to God, and he will come near to you'. Play some quiet worship music and encourage the children to think about the story and spend some time listening to God and simply enjoying his presence.

9 Jesus and Peter Walk on Water

Aim

- To discover that nothing is impossible for Jesus.

Opening Activity

Ask the children to find a space, then explain that you want them to mime walking round the room in different ways. But when you clap your hands, they must freeze like statues and wait for the next instruction. When everyone is ready, shout out the following instructions one by one:

You're walking along a very muddy path … uphill … on a frozen lake … on drawing pins … on a bouncy trampoline … through long grass … along a sandy beach … and, finally, you're walking on water.

At this point, no doubt, some children will tell you that walking on water is impossible! Explain that in this week's story we are going to hear how Peter did just that.

Bible Story

Matthew 14:22–33: use 'Mime Time', section 2:8.

Application

Make a 'Gobsmacked Message Card', section 4:6; or a Stand-up Card, section 4:7, with the caption 'Nothing is impossible for Jesus'. While the children are working, point out that in the story Peter was fine while he kept his eyes on Jesus. But when he started to think about the wind and the waves, he started to sink. Sometimes we are just like Peter: we think about the size of the problem and forget to ask Jesus to give us the strength to cope. Moving to a new town, going to a different school, making new friends, understanding a difficult subject at school, dealing with bullying, can all seem impossible. But with Jesus there to give us strength and help us cope, nothing is impossible.

Response

When Peter started to sink in the water, he turned to Jesus and asked for his help. Invite the children to write 'Please help' prayers on a prayer wall, section 9:10.

10 Easter – Doubting Thomas

Aim

- To rejoice with Thomas because Jesus came back to life and is still alive today.

Opening Activity

Take a large sheet of paper and divide it into two columns. Draw a sad face at the top of one column and a happy face at the top of the other. Ask the children to tell you some of the things that make them feel sad, eg bullying, feeling lonely, the death of a pet, when a friend moves away, a bad day at school. Write these under the 'frownie' face. Then ask them what kind of things make them feel happy; write their suggestions under the smiley face, eg birthdays, the last day of term, holidays, Christmas, funny jokes, yummy chocolate cakes, good friends.

Explain that today's story is about a man called Thomas who was feeling very sad, as sad as if all the things in column one had happened to him on the same day. Thomas was miserable because his very special friend, Jesus, had died. However, something happened to make Thomas feel happy again. Let's hear the story and find out what it was.

Bible Story

John 20:19–29: use 'Changing Feelings', section 2:9.

Application

In the story we heard how Thomas was overjoyed when he discovered that Jesus had come back to life. We can share his joy because Jesus is still alive today. Make a wallpaper border, section 5:4, with the words 'We believe that Jesus died and rose again' (1 Thessalonians 4:14). Decorate your border in bright colours, with smiley faces.

Response

Make an Easter bouquet, section 9:1. Choose bright spring colours and, if possible, cut daffodil or primrose shapes. Invite the children to write a simple line of praise in the centre of their flowers, eg 'Jesus is alive! Hallelujah!', 'Jesus is risen!' or 'Praise the Lord, it's Easter!'

Bonus section

Ten Useful Templates

A number of these templates are used in other Pick 'n' Mix activities, eg the flower, the heart, the sheep, the gingerbread person and the fish.

Ten Christmas Pictures

Ten Books and Videos Worth Looking at

The following will equip you with new ideas and help you develop the skills you need to work with children in a Christian context. They are all produced by Scripture Union.

- **Become like a child**
  Kathryn Copsey
  Step inside the world of the 5s to 7s to discover the characteristics and qualities of this age group.
  ISBN 0 86201 862 5, UK price £4.95
- **Help! There's a child in my church!**
  Peter Graystone
  To help you set achievable aims and develop the necessary skills for working with 8s to 10s in church.
  ISBN 0 86201 544 8, UK price £5.25
- **A church for all ages**
  Peter Graystone
  A comprehensive book containing advice and a huge selection of resources for the occasions when adults and children worship together.
  ISBN 0 86201 895 5, UK price £6.95
- **The adventure begins**
  Terry Clutterham
  For Christian parents and church group leaders, to help overcome difficulties that under 12s have with the Bible.
  ISBN 0 86201 906 0, UK price £6.99
- **Quiz resource book**
  Richard & Mary Chewter (eds)
  Photocopiable artwork, ready-to-use quizzes and help to create your own questions. Also offers guidance on age groups and how to present quizzes in an exciting way.
  ISBN 1 85999 049 5, UK price £7.50
- **The Christmas Video**
  Three separate re-tellings of the Christmas story for different age groups. Includes free activity material.
  ISBN 1 85999 091 6, UK price £14.99
- **Good Friday and Easter Sunday**
  Two video presentations of the gospel accounts narrated with great sensitivity by Fulton Mackay.
  ISBN 1 85999 091 6, UK price £14.99
  ISBN 1 85999 142 4, UK price £14.99
- **Going Bananas!**
  Companion video to the newest of Scripture Union's holiday club programmes. Five Bible characters who 'went bananas' for God come to life before our eyes.
  ISBN 1 85999 156 4, UK price £14.99
- **Chattabox**
  Companion video to the Chattabox holiday club. Five Bible stories stunningly retold. For 7s to 11s from church and non-church backgrounds.
  ISBN 1 85999 045 2, UK price £14.99
- **Newshounds – Location Report**
  Companion video to the Newshounds holiday club. Jake Newshound and Anne O'Pinion investigate the life, death and resurrection of Jesus, based on Luke's Gospel.
  ISBN 1 85999 151 3, UK price £14.99

Videos are an excellent way to grab children's attention and engage their imagination. A video can provide a professional storyteller who relates a Bible story in a lively and engaging manner. Of course, a video is no substitute for you, the leader. A video can't interact with the children, play games with them or answer their questions! However, once in a while it can make a welcome and refreshing change and provide you with a starting point from which you can further explore the Bible story.

For a catalogue of Scripture Union books and video resources, write to the Sales & Marketing Dept, 207–209 Queensway, Bletchley, MK2 2EB, tel 01908 856000.

Ten Jokes for the Young at Heart

Jokes make an excellent programme filler. Why not make your own Giggle Box? Cover a shoe box in bright coloured paper and cut a hole in the top. Let the youngsters post their jokes into the box and whenever there is a gap in the programme take out one or two and read them out. You might like to encourage the youngsters to give each joke a mark out of ten on the groan factor scale! Here are a few jokes to get you started, the first five are all based on biblical names:

Knock, Knock! *Who's there?*
Noah. *Noah who?*
No-ah don't know who you are either!

Knock, Knock! *Who's there?*
Amos. *Amos who?*
A mosquito!

Knock, Knock! *Who's there?*
Anna. *Anna who?*
Anna 'nother mosquito!

Knock, Knock! *Who's there?*
Luke. *Luke who?*
Luke through the keyhole and you'll find out!

Knock, Knock! *Who's there?*
Isaac. *Isaac who?*
Isaa' comin in!

Q: What's purple and conquered the world?
A: Alexander the grape!

Q: How did the mother know that an elephant had been in the fridge?
A: She saw the footprints in the butter!

Q: Why can't a car play football?
A: Because it only has one boot!

Q: How many elephants can you get in a mini?
A: Four, two in the front and two in the back!
Q: How many giraffes can you get in a mini?
A: None, it's already full of elephants!

Q: How do you start a teddy bear race?
A: Ready teddy go!